Formerly
New Directions for
Mental Health Services

Editor-in-Chief

NEW DIRECTIONS FOR YOUTH DEVELOPMENT

Theory
Practice
Research

winter | 2002

Youth Participation
Improving Institutions and Communities

Benjamin Kirshner
Jennifer L. O'Donoghue
Milbrey McLaughlin

issue
editors

JOSSEY-BASS
A Wiley Imprint
www.josseybass.com

YOUTH PARTICIPATION: IMPROVING INSTITUTIONS AND COMMUNITIES
Benjamin Kirshner, Jennifer L. O'Donoghue, Milbrey McLaughlin (eds.)
New Directions for Youth Development, No. 96, Winter 2002
Gil G. Noam, Editor-in-Chief

Microfilm copies of issues and articles are available in 16mm and 35mm, as well as microfiche in 105mm, through University Microfilms Inc., 300 North Zeeb Road, Ann Arbor, Michigan 48106-1346.

ISSN 1533-8916 (print)   ISSN 1537-5781 (online)

NEW DIRECTIONS FOR YOUTH DEVELOPMENT is part of The Jossey-Bass Psychology Series and is published quarterly by Wiley Subscription Services, Inc., A Wiley Company, at Jossey-Bass, 989 Market Street, San Francisco, California 94103-1741. Periodicals postage paid at San Francisco, California, and at additional mailing offices. Postmaster: Send address changes to New Directions for Youth Development, Jossey-Bass, 989 Market Street, San Francisco, California 94103-1741.

SUBSCRIPTIONS cost $75.00 for individuals and $149.00 for institutions, agencies, and libraries. Prices subject to change. Refer to the order form at the back of this issue.

EDITORIAL CORRESPONDENCE should be sent to the Editor-in-Chief, Dr. Gil G. Noam, Harvard Graduate School of Education, Larsen Hall 601, Appian Way, Cambridge, MA 02138 or McLean Hospital, 115 Mill Street, Belmont, MA 02478.

Cover photograph by Getty Images.

Jossey-Bass Web address: www.josseybass.com

Contents

Editor-in-Chief's Notes: The meaning of youth participation   *1*
   Gil G. Noam

Issue Editors' Notes   *5*
   Benjamin Kirshner, Jennifer L. O'Donoghue, Milbrey McLaughlin

Executive Summary   *9*

1. Introduction: Moving youth participation forward   *15*
   Jennifer L. O'Donoghue, Benjamin Kirshner, Milbrey McLaughlin
   There is much to be learned in the emerging field of youth participation.
   Examining existing challenges is critical to achieve effective and meaning-
   ful engagement of young people.

2. From assets to agents of change: Social justice, organizing, and
   youth development   *27*
   Shawn Ginwright, Taj James
   Youth development strategies can be strengthened by efforts that help
   youth become agents of change to meet pressing problems in their
   communities.

3. Youth conferences as a context for engagement   *47*
   S. Mark Pancer, Linda Rose-Krasnor, Lisa D. Loiselle
   Youth conferences bring youth from across Canada together to wrestle
   with social issues and develop strategies for community development.

4. Building young people's public lives: One foundation's
   strategy   *65*
   Robert F. Sherman
   Youth are capable of making a significant impact on problems in their
   communities and developing a sense of their potential as civic actors in the
   process—with the right support.

5. Moving youth participation into the classroom: Students
   as allies   *83*
   Barbara Cervone, Kathleen Cushman
   Student voices inform us about the key ways that teachers can make their
   classrooms safe for meaningful participation.

6. Youth evaluating programs for youth: Stories of
   Youth IMPACT   *101*

   A report written by youth evaluators describes their process and findings.
   Interviews with youth evaluators and a city department director describe
   key lessons from the process.

Index   *119*

Editor-in-Chief's Notes

The meaning of youth participation

AS AN ADOLESCENT, I went to a school in Europe that was firmly built on the progressive and humanistic ideals of Dewey, Geheeb, and Schweitzer. In this setting, which believed in infusing the voices of youth into the life and learning of the school, few goals were more important than the hard work of democratic self-governance. Students had their own parliament with committees and chairs, and their decisions counted in all major aspects of the school community's life. But one day, a serious shadow was cast over this oasis of student decision making.

A cohort of youth wanted to test the limits of their voice. What from an American perspective might seem ridiculous became a major standoff between adolescents and adults: the students voted to introduce sweaters with a school logo as an expression of their pride and belonging. Many of the faculty members viewed this plan as a return to uniforms, something youth all over fascist Europe were forced to wear. An irreconcilable schism broke open that was finally "settled" by a veto from the head of school, who decided against the school sweaters. This move was, in fact, constitutional under the rules of the school and its democratic system. The decision, however, had serious reverberations. The next two graduating classes felt more alienated and cynical, distrusting the authenticity of the very democratic rules that the school wanted students to embrace. The prevailing feeling was that if "push comes to shove," the adults make the significant decisions.

Of course, the school and its institutions survived this event, and the young people who were disappointed did not become

NEW DIRECTIONS FOR YOUTH DEVELOPMENT, NO. 96, WINTER 2002 © WILEY PERIODICALS, INC.

disillusioned in democracy for the rest of their lives. But there are important lessons to be learned. Youth participation is a commitment we make to young people. Their idealism, energy, and ingenuity are a gift to us, and we need to treat it as such. Managing the parameters of their voice, the boundaries of their decision making, is essential so as not to let their expressions of power and will deteriorate into alienation and disinterest. There are few things that are more disheartening than the dismissal from above of a group's hard work. The only way to protect from such disappointments is to be very clear what is being sought: Advice? Ideas? Decisions? Participation? Each one of these goals is a form of "youth participation," but the underlying understandings and commitments are quite different.

We all have to learn how to be very clear about these parameters as we engage with youth. We cannot play with youth voices, accept them as long as they fit our programs and communities and reject them when they do not. To engage in dialogue and joint decision making means to be willing to change the adult ways and experiment with new solutions. If we are not willing to receive the ideas and projects of young people, it is almost better not to solicit their advice. Youth participation is not a technique; it is a way of conceptualizing youth development, a willingness to engage in an intergenerational dialogue. This volume of *New Directions for Youth Development* shows us the many exciting approaches to youth participation. The issue editors, Benjamin Kirshner, Jennifer L. O'Donoghue, and Milbrey McLaughlin, have assembled an impressive group of chapter authors who contribute to the topic from different vantage points. This volume has the potential to become a classic contribution to this emerging field. It can help shape the ways research is conducted and the steps communities and organizations can take to empower young people.

Ultimately, youth participation is not only about creativity and belief in youth. It is also about power. How much decision making are we willing to let grow out of the voicing of concerns? Some foundations have gone quite far and provided funds for young people themselves to make grants. Some after-school programs let high school students be very active in decision making and planning. But most organizations still feel insecure about how to deal with the desire of young people to have some power and to be participants in shaping their surroundings. My advice here is simple: you will need to experiment and find out what works for your organization and your group of adolescents. But be very clear from the outset what you are seeking and who has a voice about what. Do not pretend that people can participate if participation does not have meaning. Invite the voices if you are willing to listen to them.

I know this advice might seem quite trivial, but as my example from my own school shows, it is not. The fact is, my teachers and school head felt strongly about not having sweaters with logos because it reminded them of Nazi uniforms. This was a deeply held conviction, and youth can respect such fundamental positions in adults. But what was not legitimate was to wait until after the vote to introduce a veto, instead of stating very clearly beforehand that the adults were not willing to take this step and were also not willing to have the students make this decision. A vote implied that the school agreed that the students had the right to make this decision. The fact is that they did not. Alienation came not from clarity about something the adults were not willing to let youth make decisions about; it came from pretending they were willing until the results did not fit their perspective. Or perhaps it was not so neat, and the democratic process only clarified the boundaries of what the adults were willing to accept. In any case, it serves as a reminder to adults that youth deserve not only to be invited into decision making but to know the true meaning of their participation.

Gil G. Noam
Editor-in-Chief

Issue Editors' Notes

YOUTH PARTICIPATION is defined in multiple ways; we understand it as *a constellation of activities that empower adolescents to take part in and influence decision making that affects their lives and to take action on issues they care about.* As this volume of *New Directions for Youth Development* demonstrates, the range of these activities can be broad and their impact—on individuals, communities, and institutions—deep.

Collectively, the chapters in this volume share the view that youth participation is a central feature of youth development. The authors provide evidence for the notion that adults must take youth seriously, not just as potential future actors but as actors now. Exploring youth participation in diverse settings, ranging from classroom organization to political organizing, they deflate myths that apathy, laziness, and "storm and stress" are necessary features of adolescence. At the same time, they avoid a cheerleading approach, opting instead for a careful analysis of the possibilities for youth participation and the challenges that exist, a topic taken up specifically in Chapter One.

Chapters Two through Four together form a cluster, taking on issues of civic participation and democratic education, a major theme in the youth participation field. In Chapter Two, Shawn Ginwright and Taj James argue that youth development advocates must see young people not just as assets but as agents of change. In recognizing that most youth of color grow up in social contexts characterized by oppression and inequity, they outline strategies that youth organizing groups are adopting to engage youth of color in political

We acknowledge the support of the John W. Gardner Center for Youth and Their Communities for the development and production of this issue.

NEW DIRECTIONS FOR YOUTH DEVELOPMENT, NO. 96, WINTER 2002 © WILEY PERIODICALS, INC.

participation and social change. The social justice youth development approach they articulate joins key youth development principles with a social-ecological analysis of the context of youth's lives.

Mark Pancer, Linda Rose-Krasnor, and Lisa Loiselle, also concerned with the political participation of youth, take a somewhat different approach, focusing on the more formal setting of youth conferences for bringing young people into conversation with government officials at the national level. In Chapter Three, they describe a process by which youth from across Canada come together to talk about social issues and brainstorm solutions. Drawing on research with the participants in these settings, the authors articulate a model for describing processes of youth engagement in terms of initiating and sustaining factors.

In Chapter Four, Robert Sherman describes one foundation's response to the emerging interest expressed by youth in civic activism and engagement. He outlines the strategy that the Surdna Foundation has taken to support youth organizing and provides examples of the work that youth have done. The chapter reminds us that youth participation is not merely about becoming part of adult institutions, but also about critiquing and transforming institutions that are not functioning effectively for youth and their families.

Youth participation is not just about politics or community-based organizations. Observers note that too often youth participation efforts focus on out-of-school settings or after-school programs, even though young people spend most of their time in school. In Chapter Five, Barbara Cervone and Kathleen Cushman apply youth participation principles to their research looking at students' experiences in public school. The authors highlight youth voices in order to shed light on the features of classroom organization and teacher relationships that support youth's desire to participate and learn.

This volume closes with a contribution from Youth IMPACT, a program that trains young people to evaluate city-funded services for youth in San Francisco. After the first study was completed in 2001, its recommendations were incorporated into the funding criteria for city-supported youth programs. In Chapter Six, we present excerpts from their 2001 report, describing their process and key findings, as well as interviews with current youth members and the former adult city department director. The interviews shed light on the key elements of this partnership between adults and youth that help it to be effective.

These chapters together contribute to our understanding of what youth participation is and can become. Youth participation truly is a new direction for youth development, one that requires both sympathetic support and careful scrutiny.

Benjamin Kirshner
Jennifer L. O'Donoghue
Milbrey McLaughlin
Issue Editors

BENJAMIN KIRSHNER *is a doctoral student in adolescent development at the Stanford University School of Education.*

JENNIFER L. O'DONOGHUE *is a doctoral student in educational administration and policy analysis at the Stanford University School of Education.*

MILBREY MCLAUGHLIN *is David Jacks Professor of Education and Public Policy at Stanford University, executive director of the John W. Gardner Center for Youth and Their Communities, and codirector of the Center for Research on the Context of Teaching.*

Executive Summary

Chapter One: Introduction: Moving youth participation forward

Jennifer L. O'Donoghue, Benjamin Kirshner,
Milbrey McLaughlin

Youth participation has garnered broad and multidisciplinary support in recent years among researchers and practitioners. Yet questions remain in this developing field about what participation looks like, how it functions, and where it takes place. This introductory chapter provides a sketch of the state of the field of youth participation and looks at the ways in which a lack of empirical evidence and understanding can fuel myths around youth engagement. Given a broader context that remains dominated by proponents of adult-controlled policies and practices for youth, it is critical to identify these myths and their associated challenges in order to build a convincing, evidence-rich case for the merits of engaging young people in organizational or public decision making and action.

Chapter Two: From assets to agents of change: Social justice, organizing, and youth development

Shawn Ginwright, Taj James

In unprecedented numbers, young people throughout the country are joining together to demand a voice in the decisions that affect their lives and their communities. In the process, they are transforming policies and making institutions more accountable through

NEW DIRECTIONS FOR YOUTH DEVELOPMENT, NO. 96, WINTER 2002 © WILEY PERIODICALS, INC.

consciousness raising, organizing, and political action. This chapter examines recent examples of youth political action and uses them to illustrate themes of youth political development and empowerment. It broadens the traditionally individual focus of youth development by using a social ecology approach to provide a brief overview of the political, economic, and cultural contexts in which youth development and political participation occur. It also examines frameworks for political participation and identifies commonalities and divergences between them. As well, it explicates the conditions for successfully engaging youth in political empowerment and examines the individual, community, and institutional impacts of youth participation in political organizing.

Chapter Three: Youth conferences as a context for engagement

S. Mark Pancer, Linda Rose-Krasnor, Lisa D. Loiselle

Youth conferences can be effective means for engaging youth in the life of their schools, communities, and nation, bringing benefits not only to youth themselves but also to the community, which gains through the energy, ideas, and values that they contribute. For the past ten years, youth from diverse backgrounds and geographical locations across Canada have come together in national conferences to express their feelings about significant social issues, talk with other youth about their own experiences, and develop policies, strategies, and programs that they can bring back to their communities to help better the lives of youth. These conferences also bring youth into direct contact with government decision makers, allowing for an exchange of ideas and information that can benefit both youth and government.

This chapter provides a definition and conceptual framework for youth engagement that articulates factors at individual and systems levels that initiate and sustain youth participation. It discusses the developmental outcomes associated with engagement and offers a description and analysis of how youth conferences foster the engagement process.

Chapter Four: Building young people's public lives: One foundation's strategy

Robert F. Sherman

Foundations are awakening to the untapped potential of serious, policy-focused community change efforts led by teenagers and young adults. This chapter lays out the background questions, a point of view, and programmatic strategies developed by one foundation seeking to support young people in taking direct action to improve their own lives and communities.

The Effective Citizenry Program of the Surdna Foundation has evolved a two-pronged funding approach. Grants support (1) young people leading and taking direct action for policy-focused community change (consistent with group identities and collective intentions), and (2) building the infrastructure to make that direct action as effective as possible (by supporting intermediary organizations that strengthen the work of community-based activist youth groups).

The chapter explores several assumptions underlying Surdna's grant-making choices. First, youth development theory and research teach that civic involvement with meaningful community problems helps achieve overall development goals. A compelling case can be made for why adolescents and young adults are constitutionally prepared to take collective, values-driven leadership around the issues that concern them most. Second, institutions evolve substantially when young people lead their own organizations. Finally, significant progress can be made to change negative conditions within institutions or communities. Examples from the Surdna Foundation's grant making provide illustration.

Chapter Five: Moving youth participation into the classroom: Students as allies

Barbara Cervone, Kathleen Cushman

A growing body of research documents the benefits to youth and adults of valuing the participation, ideas, and contributions of young people. But this underlying principle of the youth development field seems curiously distant from the daily goings-on of most American high schools.

How can we move the idea of youth participation beyond the student councils, clubs, and extracurricular activities, where it is traditionally sequestered, and into daily classroom exchange? How can student voices breathe new meaning into the phrase *class participation* or transform student-teacher interactions into partnerships of mutual respect rather than skirmishes for control?

In the spring of 2002, Kathleen Cushman, a writer with the organization What Kids Can Do, worked with forty urban high school students in a series of writing and interview sessions to seek their answers to these questions. What these students care about most, they tell us, is their relationships with teachers. They yearn for teachers eager to engage them in a scrupulous give-and-take grounded in mutual respect and trust. In return, they offer what we most want them to give: a determination to meet challenges, behave generously, and do their best work.

This chapter presents students' first-person accounts, unvarnished and at times disturbing, of their daily classroom encounters. Their experiences not only provide teachers with guidance on how to reach adolescent learners but illustrate what youth-adult partnerships in the classroom might look.

Chapter Six: Youth evaluating programs for youth: Stories of Youth IMPACT

In 2000, the San Francisco Department of Children Youth and Their Families (DCYF) initiated a youth-led evaluation of city-funded services for young people. The youth research team that took shape, Youth IMPACT, conducted an evaluation of forty youth-serving programs in the city, resulting in a set of criteria that the city now uses to assess the quality of future grant applications. Now in its third year, Youth IMPACT continues to work with the city to assess the quality of resources for children and youth.

This chapter presents excerpts from the report written by members of Youth IMPACT in 2001, an interview with four current members of Youth IMPACT, and an interview with the former director of DCYF. Together, these speak to the power of youth participation, which influenced not only the young people involved but also community programs and the very structure of public institutions. The time and energy devoted to making Youth IMPACT work was rewarded with improved services, new strategies for grant making, greater government effectiveness, and youth empowerment. Youth IMPACT demonstrates that youth, in partnership with adults, have something powerful to contribute.

Given the emerging interest among researchers, practitioners, and policymakers in youth participation, it is important to examine and assess carefully the promise and challenges of youth engagement.

1

Introduction: Moving youth participation forward

Jennifer L. O'Donoghue, Benjamin Kirshner, Milbrey McLaughlin

FIVE YOUTH from the San Francisco Bay Area recently joined twenty-five other young people and over one hundred adults at an international conference on the United Nations Convention on the Rights of the Child. "It was the most un-youth-friendly place," explained one young woman. "Every day we woke up early and spent hours listening to adults lecture about the experiences of youth. There was no time for us to talk to anyone, no time to move around, and when we tried to tell them about our feelings, they didn't really listen. Nothing really changed—until the last day when *we* finally got to do *our* presentation. One of the adults tried to come up and facilitate our question-and-answer period, and we just said, 'No, thank you. We're prepared to do this for ourselves. Sit down please.' I don't think the adults really got it until then."[1]

The concept of youth participation, whether under the name of youth voice, decision making, empowerment, engagement, or participation, has become a hot topic. The United Nations Convention on the Rights of the Child (CRC), the most widely ratified treaty in history, made participation a fundamental right of all young people.[2] Advocates and researchers of youth development point to the developmental benefits of youth involvement in decision

NEW DIRECTIONS FOR YOUTH DEVELOPMENT, NO. 96, WINTER 2002 © WILEY PERIODICALS, INC.

making and public engagement.[3] Youth participation has been linked to greater organizational sustainability and effectiveness[4] and, on a macrolevel, national democratic, social, and economic development.[5] Not surprisingly, then, the idea of youth participation has garnered broad support across a range of disciplines and practices. However, the frustrations experienced by the young people cited at the start of this chapter point to a central issue within this growing field: even adults and youth with the best intentions struggle with just what youth participation means. What does it look like? How does it happen?

Participation is a broad term, encompassing several dimensions. The CRC defines youth participation as freedom of expression on issues affecting young people.[6] Participation can also be organized around three general themes: access to social, political, and economic spheres; decision making within organizations that influence one's life; and planning and involvement in public action.[7] For the purposes of this chapter, we understand youth participation as *a constellation of activities that empower adolescents to take part in and influence decision making that affects their lives and to take action on issues they care about.*

This introductory chapter provides a sketch of the state of the field of youth participation, reviewing what is known about what participation looks like, how it functions, and where it takes place.[8] As a developing field, the answer to many of these questions is "not enough." This lack of evidence and understanding can potentially fuel myths around youth participation. We address four of these myths, pointing to some of the important questions to think about in achieving meaningful youth engagement.

Where we are: Youth participation in research and practice

Youth development researchers have noted a shift in youth work in the past two decades from prevention (programs designed to treat and prevent the problems of "at-risk" youth) to preparation (building skills and supporting broader development for all youth) to participation and power sharing (actively engaging young people as partners in organizational and public decision making).[9] These shifts represent a broadening of focus from looking solely at individual-level outcomes to also examining the organizational and community-level impacts of youth participation.

With this expanding focus, efforts to take youth participation seriously have extended beyond traditional youth development activities to embrace youth involvement in other areas. For example, as Chapter Six of this volume illustrates, researchers, policymakers, and program evaluators are beginning to involve young people as research partners, working to understand better the lives of youth and the institutions that influence them.[10] Internationally, young people have been central to grassroots social, environmental, and economic change movements,[11] a pattern that, as discussed in Chapters Two and Four, is beginning to show up in the United States as well. Moreover, many nonprofit and youth organizations have come to embrace the notion that youth voices should be part of organizational decision making,[12] and young people have begun to be engaged in school reform efforts.[13]

Most observers agree, however, that the corresponding research on youth participation—its prerequisites, organizational features, current scope, and impacts—remains in the early stages. In part, this reflects a lack of consensus on conceptual frameworks and definitions,[14] especially ones that take into account the influence of local contexts. Effective approaches to youth participation in Brazil, for example, have been shown to be less successful when implemented in the United States because of differing policy and organizational contexts.[15] Broad and meaningful participation seems to require a larger policy context in which the voices of youth are listened to and taken seriously, and we still have much to learn about the multiple ways in which context influences local efforts.

Similarly, little consensus exists on where youth participation most appropriately or effectively occurs. The majority of work around youth engagement has tended to focus on the experiences of young people in community-based or nongovernmental organizations.[16] These organizations often do not face the same sets of constraints as public institutions, and as a result, they may offer young people the type of alternative spaces that they need to reflect critically and build capacity for action. Youth organizing efforts are also typically based in community, whether in formal organizations or less-formal grassroots movements, and often work outside the system or act in opposition to public institutions. While acknowledging the strength and importance of such efforts, researchers and practitioners have begun to point to the need to bring youth participation to public institutions as well, working to create change from within. Many consider youth participation in schools, for example, critical to creating sustainable and significant change.[17] As Deborah Alvarez-Rodriguez notes in Chapter Six, greater youth participation in public institutions can lead to substantive improvements in government effectiveness.

Youth participation, then, occurs in multiple settings and across multiple levels, from local to national and global. The common denominator across these levels is that if participation is to be effective, it must become embedded in institutions and processes that influence young people's everyday lives.

Research on outcomes for youth and organizations has provided broad evidence of the benefits of youth participation. Some promising evidence about youth outcomes stems from research on student motivation in classrooms, in which participation in decision making has been correlated with greater effort, intrinsic interest, and more effective learning strategies.[18] Youth development practitioners also have found that participation is an effective strategy for engaging youth, especially older high school students, who typically avoid youth organizations that do not give them a voice in decision making or planning.[19] Such engagement has been found to have an impact on the host organizations, which report that youth participation in decision making leads to changes in the organizational climate and a deeper commitment by adults to youth development principles.[20] Finally, meaningful participation is said to foster democratic habits in youth, such as tolerance, healthy disagreement, self-expression, and cooperation.[21] Recent work studying community impact, although challenging to measure, has begun to document the ways in which youth participation has led to meaningful community change as well.[22]

Despite these emerging empirical examples, the field is still developing. It will be important in the coming years to build on these lines of research to gain a deeper and more nuanced understanding of the necessary conditions that support youth participation and the benefits that can accrue to participants and the wider community. We know little, for example, about the kinds of roles that adults play to support effective youth engagement. In addition, there exists little understanding of the organizational features of spaces that encourage youth participation. And while research efforts are beginning to focus on developmental outcomes for youth, still needed is a richer base of evidence demonstrating the impact of participation on both young people and the communities of which they are a part.

Myths of youth participation

Although youth participation is an international phenomenon, it is also closely linked to local context. As such, we focus our lens here on the current policy climate in North America, which is often divided between defenders of more adult-controlled policies and practices for youth, on one hand, and adherents of youth participation, on the other. The first group tends to see youth as problems to be fixed or dependents to be taken care of. Its proponents rarely view youth as resources to be engaged in creating social and community change.

In the United States, these youth participation naysayers play a powerful role in shaping discussions of youth and youth policy. For example, in 2000, California voters passed Proposition 21, a controversial juvenile crime ballot initiative that increases the penalties for juvenile offenses and the range of cases that can be tried in adult courts.[23] Policies such as this reflect and reinforce perceptions of young people as dangerous and disengaged. Studies showing the intractability of these negative constructions of youth in the minds of adults demonstrate the challenge of creating a broad movement of youth participation in the United States.[24]

In contrast, there are many who have wholeheartedly embraced the notion of youth participation, sometimes promoting an overly romantic notion of youth involvement. We refer to this often sentimental position as one held by the "true believer." Themes of voice and participation echo rich traditions in progressive education that value the autonomy of the child and the importance of appealing to his or her passions and interests. Yet in the struggle to convince others of the rights and abilities of young people to engage in organizational or public decision making and action, careful and critical understanding of youth participation is required.

As the idea of youth participation gains steam, the field is at a critical juncture. It is more important than ever before to identify and uncover the myths surrounding youth participation in order to build a convincing, evidence-rich case for its merits. We outline four such myths and discuss key issues facing supporters of youth participation.

Myth 1: Youth participation is accomplished by placing one youth on a board or committee

Many school boards, city councils, and boards of directors of nonprofit organization have begun to create space for youth representatives. Although this marks a potentially important first step in opening the door to youth voice and participation, it also may limit the involvement of young people. Such a conception carries with it two related problems: tokenism and exclusivity.

Inserting one or a few youth into an adult-created and adult–driven process runs the risk of involving youth as tokens or "decorations,"[25] precluding any opportunity for meaningful participation or substantive influence. An authentic process is not one that is determined solely by adults. Rather, youth need multiple spaces for engagement. In this way, youth participation efforts can tap into the interests, passions, and skills of young people. Alternative points of entry can also open the space for youth to redesign and recreate the institutions that influence their lives.

In addition to the risk of tokenism, involving a few youth as representatives of larger groups may result in exclusivity, whereby only the most privileged or skilled youth are chosen to participate. Theorists of public participation have raised important questions to consider in thinking about authentic youth involvement.[26] Central among these are questions about who participates that point to the need to work intentionally for broad and inclusive participation. This means building structures, practices, and cultures that support the participation of youth who may not come from privileged backgrounds or who may not yet have the skills to participate effectively. Creating inclusive participation also means overcoming the idea of representativeness. Although youth participation implies that youth share common interests, it is important to remember how multiple and diverse their backgrounds and experiences are. Young people engage with the public world as individuals, not as representatives of all youth, African American youth, or gay youth, for example.

Myth 2: Youth participation means that adults surrender their roles as guides and educators

Whereas the problem with myth 1 lies in its limited assumptions about the involvement of youth, the challenge with myth 2 lies in limited assumptions about the involvement of adults. Too often, discussions of youth participation are silent about the roles that adults must play as supporters and educators. The field will benefit from thoughtful attention to these roles because they are unlike those typically played by adults who work with youth and a necessary feature of successful youth participation efforts.

Youth participation projects are often one of the few arenas in which adults socialize youth into practices and habits of the professional world. For example, in Chapter Six, Deborah Alvarez-Rodriguez points out her role as a sympathetic critic of the members of Youth IMPACT, a youth-led evaluation program in San Francisco. If youth made a presentation and the audience did not understand what they were saying or if young people did not take their professional obligations seriously, she gave them feedback to help them improve. In other words, supporters of youth participation must be open to the unique voices and contributions of youth, but they also must help youth learn how to recognize the norms of the public arena or the specific practices of the field in which they hope to participate. This is not so that youth will merely adopt these norms, but so that they can be effective in shaping broader arenas.

Adults also often play roles as critical guides, especially in projects that are oriented toward civic participation or political activism. What if there were a youth empowerment project where students decided to exclude someone because of that person's ethnicity or sexual orientation? Or, in a more likely scenario, what if youth wished to make an impact on their community but lacked knowledge of political processes or a critical consciousness about deep-seated public problems? Most would agree that such projects would be flawed efforts at youth participation. Adults play critical roles in providing guidance and connecting youth with needed information and resources.

Myth 3: Adults are ready for youth participation

An assumption of adult readiness brings some of the most intractable problems to youth participation efforts. As seen in the episode that opened this chapter, even the best-intentioned adults may not yet understand what youth participation means. Adults need to adapt to youth participation as much as (if not more than) youth do. This requires ongoing training and development of adults in how best to support youth and fulfill their roles as adult allies. Successful youth-adult partnerships recognize the importance of supporting adult learning and change to nurture effective youth participation.[27]

A greater challenge, however, may come from the need for adults to change their frames, that is, their understandings of youth and how to work with them. Even in institutions created to develop and serve youth, young people often face ambivalence from adults about their ability to participate in real-world decision making and action.[28] As one young person put it, adults do not see youth as "actual people" able to effect change in the world. True participation, then, means changing deeply held beliefs of adults—not just about age but also constructions around race, ethnicity, and class. At its most basic level, it requires a "willingness to be changed."[29]

Myth 4: Youth are ready to participate; they just need the opportunity

Just as adults need support and training, authentic youth engagement requires that young people be given the time and space to develop the skills they need to participate effectively. This does not mean that youth need to learn now and participate later, but rather that they have ongoing training and support during the participation process. This training includes domain-specific skills. Projects that involve youth in program evaluation, for example, need to train youth in research methods, such as interviewing or data analysis, which typically are not part of a regular school curriculum. Youth preparation also includes the development of broader skills. To engage meaningfully in decision making, youth (like adults) may need workshops and practice in facilitation, public speaking, and collaborative processes. Finally, youth too may need experiences that alter their frames about what is possible for young people. Involvement with real-world issues and projects where they can see the larger community or public impact may be the best way for youth to learn what they are capable of.

Moving forward

The myths articulated here represent key barriers to meaningful youth participation. They highlight the need for honest discussion and analysis around issues of power. Are adults prepared to involve youth in meaningful ways? Are they prepared to look critically at patterns of privilege and exclusion that cut across age, race, ethnicity, class, gender, sexual orientation, and ability? How will they build structures and processes that work to overcome these? Are they ready to change, taking on roles as allies and partners rather than just directors or instructors? Equally important, are youth prepared to take on their roles as decision makers and public actors? Do they have access to the necessary knowledge and skills? Answering these questions will be crucial to understanding and strengthening youth participation efforts.

Notes

1. Anecdote taken from researcher field notes, Aug. 22, 2002.

2. To date, 191 countries have ratified the Convention on the Rights of the Child. Only two countries have not: Somalia and the United States.

3. See, for example, Hart, R. (1992). *Children's participation: From tokenism to citizenship.* Florence, Italy: UNICEF, International Child Development Centre; Hart, R., Daiute, C., & Iltus, S. (1997). Developmental theory and children's participation in community organizations. *Social Justice, 24*(3), 33–63; Pittman, K., Ferber, T., & Irby, M. (2000). *Youth as effective citizens.* Takoma Park, MD: International Youth Foundation—US.

4. Zeldin, S., McDaniel, A. K., Topitzes, D., & Calvert, M. (2000). *Youth in decision-making: A study of the impacts of youth on adults and organizations.* Chevy Chase, MD: National 4-H Council; Rajani, R. (2000). *The participation rights of adolescents: A strategic approach* (Working Paper). New York: United Nations Children's Fund.

5. Rajani (2000).

6. Hart (1992).

7. Tolman, J., & Pittman, K. (2001). *Youth acts, community impacts: Stories of youth engagement with real results.* Takoma Park, MD: Forum for Youth Investment, International Youth Foundation.

8. For a more complete review, see Hart (1992); Rajani (2000); Irby, M., Ferber, T., & Pittman, K. (2001). *Youth action: Youth contributing to communities, communities supporting youth.* Takoma Park, MD: Forum for Youth Investment, International Youth Foundation.

9. Pittman, Ferber, & Irby (2000).

10. See also Kirshner, B., O'Donoghue, J., & McLaughlin, M. (forthcoming). Youth-led research collaboration: Bringing youth voice to the research process. In J. Mahoney, J. Eccles, & R. Larson (Eds.), *After-school activities: Contexts of development.* Mahwah, NJ: Erlbaum.

11. See, for example, Brandao, C. (1998). The landmark achievements of Brazil's social movement for children's rights. *New Designs for Youth Development, 14*(3). Available at: www.cydjournal.org/newdesigns/ND_ 98fall; Espinosa, M. F., & Schwab, M. (1997). Working children in Ecuador mobilize for change. *Social Justice, 24*(3), 64–70; Hart, R., & Schwab, M. (1997). Children's rights and the building of democracy: A dialogue on the international movement for children's participation. *Social Justice, 24*(3), 177–191.

12. Zeldin et al. (2000).

13. Mitra, D. (2002). *Makin' it real: Involving youth in school reform.* Unpublished doctoral dissertation, Stanford University; Fielding, M. (2001). Students as radical agents of change. *Journal of Educational Change, 2*(2), 123–141.

14. What evidence do we have that youth participation actually works? (2001, Spring). *International Insights on Youth and Communities, 2.*

15. Brandao (1998).

16. Hart (1992); Hart et al. (1997); Ferber, T., & Pittman, K. (1999). *Finding common agendas: How young people are being engaged in community change efforts.* Takoma Park, MD: International Youth Foundation—US; Pittman et al. (2000); Tolman & Pittman (2001).

17. Hart and Schwab (1997); Rajani (2000).

18. Ames, C. (1992). Classrooms: Goals, structures, and student motivation. *Journal of Educational Psychology, 84*(3), 261–271; Eccles, J. S., Wigfield, A., & Schiefele, U. (1998). Motivation to succeed. In W. Damon (Ed.), *Handbook of child psychology, Vol. 3: Social, emotional and personality development* (pp. 1017–1094).

19. Ashley, J., Samaniego, D., & Chuen, L. (1997). How Oakland turns its back on teens: A youth perspective. *Social Justice, 24,* 170–177; McLaughlin, M. W. (2000). *Community counts: How youth organizations matter for youth development.* Washington, DC: Public Education Network.

20. Zeldin et al. (2000).

21. Hart (1992).

22. Tolman & Pittman (2001).

23. For more details, see the Web site of the California Legislative Analyst's Office: www.lao.ca.gov/initiatives/2000/21_03_2000.html.

24. Bales, S. (2000). *Reframing youth issues for public consideration and support.* Washington, DC: FrameWorks Institute.

25. Hart (1992).

26. Anderson, G. L. (1998). Toward authentic participation: Deconstructing the discourses of participatory reforms in education. *American Educational Research Journal, 35*(4), 571–603; Baksh-Soodeen, R. (2001). Lessons from the gender movement: Building a discipline to support practice. *CYD Journal, 2*(2), 61–64.

27. The HOME Project, described in some detail in Chapter Four of this volume, for example, invests significant resources in the development of adult staff. Adults create learning plans for their own work with youth and meet in adult reflection sessions to discuss their own challenges and growth in supporting youth engagement.

28. See for example, Costello, J., Toles, M., Spielberger, J., & Wynn, J. (2000). *History, ideology and structure shape the organizations that shape youth, youth development: Issues, challenges and directions.* Philadelphia: Public/Private Ventures.

29. The need for this "willingness to be changed," discussed by Deborah Alvarez-Rodriguez in Chapter Six, has also been articulated by Leslie Medine, cofounder of the HOME Project.

JENNIFER L. O'DONOGHUE *is a doctoral student in educational administration and policy analysis at the Stanford University School of Education.*

BENJAMIN KIRSHNER *is a doctoral student in adolescent development at the Stanford University School of Education.*

MILBREY MCLAUGHLIN *is David Jacks Professor of Education and Public Policy at Stanford University, executive director of the John W. Gardner Center for Youth and Their Communities, and codirector of the Center for Research on the Context of Teaching.*

Young people are joining together to demand a voice in the decisions that affect their lives. In the process, they are transforming policies and making institutions more accountable.

2

From assets to agents of change: Social justice, organizing, and youth development

Shawn Ginwright, Taj James

FEW WOULD disagree that young people today face formidable social problems. While policymakers and researchers might point to the familiar data on teen pregnancy, violence, and high school dropout rates, we believe that barriers to democratic participation are the greatest challenge facing youth. Political participation has been the cornerstone of America's democratic ideals, and yet for women and communities of color, it has come with substantial costs. Similar to blacks prior to 1954, today's young people face intense economic isolation, lack political power, and are subjected to pervasive social stigma. In response, young people throughout the country are mobilizing to demand a voice in public policy and are transforming institutions to be more accountable to their communities.

This chapter addresses three fundamental questions regarding youth political engagement. What role can youth play in forging a democratic society and creating more equitable institutions? How

NEW DIRECTIONS FOR YOUTH DEVELOPMENT, NO. 96, WINTER 2002 © WILEY PERIODICALS, INC.

can adults support sociopolitical development among youth? And what can be learned from youth organizing and its impact on the development of young people? In order to address these questions, we broaden the traditional individual focus of youth development by using a social ecology approach to provide a brief overview of the political, economic, and cultural context in which youth development and political participation occur.[1]

We focus on urban youth of color, who have largely been ignored in mainstream youth development literature. The focus on marginalized youth allows us to examine more deeply the social issues they confront and explore how they creatively respond through organizing, political education, and identity development. This approach is a model for building not only strong democratic processes, but also healthier communities and supportive environments for youth.

We identify the commonalities among youth organizing frameworks and synthesize key principles that might contribute to a general theory or model of social justice and youth development. Finally, through recent examples of youth political action, we explicate the conditions for successfully engaging youth in their political development and empowerment and examine the individual, community, and institutional impacts of youth participation in political organizing.

Youth in an ecological context: Uncovering the assault on urban youth

Talking about the assault on urban youth of color in America is somewhat like uncovering the proverbial pink elephant in the middle of a large room: everyone knows it is there, but no one talks about it. From the 1980s and into the 1990s, relatively little attention was given to the serious social conditions youth of color face in their communities. Racism, mass unemployment, pervasive violence, and police brutality pose serious threats to youth and their families. Garbarino referred to these conditions as "social toxins," a term used to represent the degree to which the social world has become poisonous to a person's well-being.[2] These toxins impede productive development for young people, who are expected to develop under these hostile conditions, and place them at a greater risk than those living in stable and safe communities. Similarly, Brooks-Gunn and colleagues found that neighborhood factors such as gun violence and police abuse, lack of health care, racist school practices, lack of jobs that pay a livable wage, and few productive after-school opportunities all present barriers to healthy development.[3]

Policymakers usually respond to these issues by blaming youth themselves or simply writing them off as a threat to civil society. This response tends to evoke public policy that conceptualizes young people as the root causes of their own problems and does not adequately address the most significant problems facing urban youth. To understand these challenges, we must look beyond the narrow parameters of individual, family, or community behavior toward the larger economic, social, and cultural forces that bear on the actions, behaviors, experiences, and choices of urban youth.

A social-ecological approach provides researchers and practitioners with a powerful lens to examine the ways in which social, political, and economic forces influence young people's development. We examine these contexts, focusing on the central question: How does context influence the development of young people of color?

Political context

In 1997, minority youth made up 34 percent of the U.S. population but 62 percent of incarcerated youth. African American youth are six times more likely to be incarcerated and receive longer sentences than their white counterparts.[4] Youth of color clearly bear the brunt of discriminatory sentencing practices. They also have few educational and economic opportunities. In California, for example, Proposition 187 denies undocumented immigrants public benefits, Proposition 209 outlaws affirmative action policies, Proposition 227 bans bilingual education, and Proposition 21 gives courts greater authority to sentence youth as young as fourteen years old as adults.

Mike Males documented how xenophobic notions of black youth, as well as fear of crime, helped to shape hostile public policy for black youth during the 1990s.[5] Despite the fact that youth crime had decreased since 1990, news stories continued to report soaring youth crime rates among black youth. Legislators responded by crafting public policy underscoring the idea that to be black, young, and poor was also to be criminal.[6] These perceptions were reinforced through public policies that reflected a growing concern for safety and the consequent increased repression through institutions such as schools, law enforcement, and juvenile justice systems.[7] From 1996 to 2002, for example, forty-three states instituted legislation that facilitated the transfer of children to adult court.

Economic context

There was a time in U.S. history when urban youth could secure a decent job with no more, or sometimes less, than a high school education. With relatively low unemployment levels in many American cities, urban youth had reason for hope and prospects for a financially stable future. Economic changes over the past twenty years have left working-class youth and their families with few job opportunities. Low-wage employment in retail and food services offers the only legitimate option for those with no more than high school diplomas.[8] The decline in both educational opportunities and livable wages forces urban youth to survive in a context with limited legitimate economic opportunities. In many urban areas, young people struggle to make ends meet by juggling two and sometimes three part-time jobs, or they often "hustle," earning money off the books through street vending.[9] The money that poor and working-class young people earn from working usually goes to support the household. These economic challenges are supported by the fact that many young people feel that completing high school means little in communities with bleak job opportunities.[10]

Social context

The policies we have described are made worse by a social context that can be best described as toxic. Youth are subjugated to serious social problems such as racism, sexism, and homophobia and are often forced to navigate these in isolation. These problems are exacerbated by the fact that traditional youth development programs rarely address the ways in which young people deal with these issues and often ignore how these issues impede their healthy development. Recently, scholars have noted that these forms of oppression can trigger depression, hopelessness, and suicidal tendencies. The trauma of persistent oppression coupled with isolation and the inability to confront and change these oppressive conditions has led scholars to believe that the presence of both can be lethal.[11]

These conditions, however, are not immutable. In fact, the capacity for individuals to challenge, resist, and change the root cause of their suffering is at the core of any democratic process. Despite the fact that young people of color grapple with these serious social conditions and have been grossly omitted from our democratic process, they still respond to injustice in their communities. Young people have always been at the vanguard for community and social change, and today's young people are no different. Following are a few examples of how young people are organizing to transform oppressive social conditions into healthy, fair, and democratic realities.

Youth in action: Examples of youth organizing

In communities around the South in the 1960s, students violated segregation laws by sitting at lunch counters in white establishments. The activity triggered a new direction in the civil rights movement and highlighted how young people are central to social change efforts. The children of South Africa, in their protests against the Bantu education system, directly confronted the government and helped to bring an end to the system of apartheid. As these examples show, the actions of young people can transform an entire nation. Today, young people around the world find themselves continuing the struggle for equality and are organizing to make the vision of equality a reality.

Many of the best examples of youth leadership come from outside the United States. Increasing inequality, poverty, and disease in Brazil led to large numbers of children forced to live on the streets without their families or any other social supports. Thousands of these street children, with the support of adult educators and youth workers, formed a movement that led them to take over the Brazilian congress and force them to adopt the United Nations Convention on the Rights of the Child.

People of color and low-income people in California have faced a decade of repressive ballot initiatives, turning back the gains made by the movements for justice and equality in the 1960s and 1970s. Youth have been in the leadership of fights against policies that would deny them education, health care, and other basic rights. At one point in this struggle, six thousand youth from all over the San Francisco Bay Area walked out of school and rallied in front of a newly built police station, across the street from a dilapidated school, to protest the underfunding of education and the overinvestment in punishment and incarceration. In response to Proposition 21, an initiative that allows youth to be tried as adults at age fourteen and criminalizes many of the normal things that young people do,[12] thousands of students again took to the streets and engaged in civil disobedience to stop the corporations that funded that proposition in California. After interrupting a corporate board meeting of one of the initiative's corporate funders and protesting outside their headquarters, the Chevron and PG&E corporations publicly renounced their support for the initiative. In all of the counties where young people mobilized in significant numbers, the initiative was defeated.

In Philadelphia, youth organizing groups are waging a struggle against corporations that want to privatize the public school system and the politicians who are allied with them. Combining sound research with direct action, youth and their adult allies have succeeded in keeping some local control over the schools, preventing the Edison corporation, one of a number of for-profit corporations looking to gain access to public dollars, from taking over the entire school system, as had been proposed.

In New York City, thousands of youth took to the streets to protest police brutality and racial profiling in the aftermath of the case of Amadou Diallo, a Haitian American who was brutalized and sodomized with the broken end of a broomstick by New York City police officers. Recently, those same groups of young people held mass rallies, incorporating hip-hop culture and music, to prevent the mayor from making deep cuts to the education budget.

These diverse examples of youth and student activism are part of a long tradition of youth taking leadership in social movements fighting for democracy and justice. During the past decade, the United States has witnessed the growth of a dynamic and diverse youth movement. This movement is being built not only through mass mobilizations of young people and their supporters, but through smaller-scale campaigns and efforts to make concrete changes in the social conditions that youth and their communities face. Students have successfully organized in communities around the country to defeat curfew laws, helped to write and pass policies protecting gay and lesbian students in school, changed the curriculum in their schools to make it more reflective of our diverse communities, and worked to stop dumping of waste and other forms of environmental racism. Young people are learning how to be citizens by revitalizing democracy.

As these examples demonstrate, the efforts of young people often lead to better public policy, stronger organizations, more relevant services, and healthier communities. But how does participation in these efforts promote the development of the youth involved? In the next section, we present some of the principles and practices that youth groups are using in transforming their environments.

Social justice youth development principles and practices

Political participation through organizing, informing the general public, and waging winnable campaigns against powerful groups holds the most promise for attaining a more inclusive democracy. In the youth development field, there has been rising interest in framing how young people engage in social justice activities.[13] Two frameworks have emerged that provide conceptual groundwork for an emerging theory about youth political engagement. The first, developed by Watts, Williams, and Jagers, offers a social-psychological discussion about the sociopolitical development of youth and the role of social oppression.[14] Using an ecological approach, they examine how young people respond within oppressive social systems and identify the process of sociopolitical development. The second framework, developed by Ginwright and Cammarota, also argues for an ecological understanding of youth development and introduces a theoretical discussion about what these authors call social justice youth development (SJYD).[15] Each model offers a unique and substantive contribution to our understanding of youth and social justice issues, but both share several principles. (See Table 2.1.)

Table 2.1. Principles, practices, and outcomes of social justice youth development

Principles	Practices	Outcomes
Analyzes power in social relationships	Political education Political strategizing Identifying power holders Reflecting about power in one's own life	Social problematizing, critical thinking, asking and answering questions related to community and social problems Development of sociopolitical awareness Youth transforming arrangements in public and private institutions by sharing power with adults
Makes identity central	Joining support groups and organizations that support identity development Reading material where one's identity is central and celebrated Critiquing stereotypes regarding one's identities	Development of pride regarding one's identity Awareness of how sociopolitical forces influence identity Feeling of being a part of something meaningful and productive The capacity to build solidarity with others who share common struggles and have shared interests

(continued)

Table 2.1. Continued

Principles	*Practices*	*Outcomes*
Promotes systemic social change	Working to end social inequality (such as racism and sexism) Refraining from activities and behaviors that are oppressive to others (for example, refusing to buy shoes made in sweatshops)	Sense of life purpose, empathy for the suffering of others, optimism about social change Liberation by ending various forms of social oppression
Encourages collective action	Involving oneself in collective action and strategies that challenge and change local and national systems and institutions Community organizing Rallies and marches Boycotts and hunger strikes Walkouts Electoral strategies	Capacity to change personal, community, and social conditions Empowerment and positive orientation toward life circumstances and events Healing from personal trauma brought on from oppression
Embraces youth culture	Celebrating youth culture in organizational culture Language Personnel Recruitment strategies	Authentic youth engagement Youth-run and youth-led organizations Effective recruitment strategies Effective external communications Engagement of extremely marginalized youth

Principles of social justice youth development

SJYD examines how urban youth contest, challenge, respond to, and negotiate the use and misuse of power in their lives. SJYD is strengthened by youth and adult allies working together with a common vision of social justice. This requires that adults take seriously their own development and that youth workers shift how they conceptualize youth development. Reaching healthy adulthood is not the only goal of SJYD; rather, it is to build a more equitable society through the engagement of critically conscious citizens through the following principles and strategies.

Analyzing power within social relationships. An analysis of power within social relationships encourages youth to examine the root causes of social problems. It also requires that they understand how the misuse of power in institutions creates systems that reproduce multiple forms of inequality. For example, such an analysis might require young people to ask, "Who has the power to influence the quality of our education?" Analysis of power often reveals hidden systems of privilege and encourages critical thinking about social problems

Making identity central. Often, inequality is linked to identity, and as a result, identity is often the starting point for youth organizing. Identities are complex ways that young people (and adults) identify themselves, as well as how they are seen by the larger society. SJYD views identity as central to developing young people because power and privilege are often granted based on identity (with the most going to white, heterosexual, middle-class men). As a result, women, people of color, and poor and gay youth often bear the brunt of social inequality. However, it is that same social inequality that brings together young people who have a shared identity to fight for social change.

Promoting systemic change. The focus on systemic change develops the capacity of young people to transform institutional practices that do not meet their needs and counters the practice of blaming the individual for the effects of structural inequalities. Young people strategize, research, and act to change school policies, state legislation, and police protocols that create and sustain inequality. Systemic change focuses on root causes of social problems and makes explicit the complex ways that various forms of oppression work together. This helps counter the low self-esteem that comes from being blamed for one's own oppression.

Encouraging collective action. Without action, there is no change. Collective action is the process of engagement that seeks to alter existing social conditions through noninstitutional means. Often, collective action emerges from groups affected by similar problems and sharing the same social justice vision. Collective action encompasses the range of strategies involved in organizing and activism, including sit-ins, rallies and marches, and boycotts. The premise is that the capacity to change oppressive social conditions lies in collective efforts, not only individual ones.

Embracing youth culture. Youth culture has been effective at communicating messages that promote social justice. It can be thought of as a set of ideas and a common worldview shared by most young people. Similar to ethnic groups that share similar cultural values, young people see the world as a place of possibilities and challenge the adult world to acknowledge its contradictions. Much of the dominant youth culture in America can also be described as hip-hop culture, often defined by a style that calls attention to the problems urban youth face on a daily basis through music, dress, and language.

Practices of social justice youth development

Many of the strategies that youth use to confront social inequality are those that have been drawn on by marginalized people throughout time to make their voices heard. Some of these reflect the particular ways that conservative political forces have chosen to target marginalized people. Following are some of the more prominent and effective strategies that young people are beginning to use, particularly in the California youth movement, which has been at the forefront of the SJYD effort. Many of the practices address multiple principles simultaneously.

Developing the tools to analyze power: Defining the problem and providing a solution. The youth organizer and founder of LISTEN Inc., Lisa Sullivan, often said that urban youth must be given the support to define their own problems and find their own solutions.[16] Much of the work that young people do in the political area is as simple as this:

Problem: Youth lack access to health care, leading to physical, psychological, emotional, and educational challenges.

Solution: Provide free health care in schools that responds to youth-defined needs.

Problem: Youth services are underused and irrelevant to youth.

Solution: Require that as a condition of funding, youth be involved in planning, implementing, and evaluating programs.

Problem: Youth from different communities have conflicts with each other in school.

Solution: Teach all groups to understand and respect their own history and culture and those of others by changing the school curriculum.

Young people are developing the capacity to critically analyze their world through political and popular education methods and learning to conduct action research, analyze social structures, and propose policy solutions. This process develops in young people an understanding of how things came to be (history) and a way to analyze how power in society is organized.

Building youth identity. Because youth rarely have opportunities to explore and develop their identities, practices that build identity yield both personal and social change. Practices that support SJYD include support groups, summer camps based on particular aspects of youth identity, and organizations devoted to identity-based advocacy. These organizations support youth through the process of healing from social ills by building their identities and providing skills to confront social problems.

Creating systemic change through collective action. Young people are developing new and creative ways to create systemic change. They are addressing social inequality through community organizing and activism; organizing marches, walkouts, and hunger strikes; developing their own ballot initiatives; putting youth voices inside the system; and using the media as tools to educate and influence. Community organizing around local issues of direct concern to youth and their communities is the most central strategy that young people are using to create systemic change.

As we have witnessed in recent corporate scandals and efforts to create campaign finance reform, corporations have a tremendous amount of power in the political process. For youth to be heard, they must often directly challenge the corporations and wealthy individuals who support hostile public policies and oppressive political agendas. During the fight against Proposition 21 in California, youth groups targeted the Hilton and Chevron corporations, which were funding the initiative, and exposed their role in promoting the agenda on incarceration. Youth forced some companies to back down and withdraw their support. After the initiative passed, youth staged a dramatic takeover of a Hilton Hotel lobby to express their outrage that rich individuals can have such a nefarious influence on the political process, sentencing a generation to less opportunity and more suffering.

In addition, youth organizing groups that have fought from outside the system to get decision makers not just to listen but to take action to support them have also worked to put youth on the inside to be allies and advocates for youth. Youth organizing groups have won campaigns to create new youth commissions and have added youth representation to school boards and state and local commissions. Across the country, these are becoming platforms from which youth fight for real voice and power.

Using youth culture to involve youth politically. Youth organizations are incorporating youth culture in their work in interesting ways. By supporting young people in making the decision about what gets done, by whom, and how, organizations are creating environments that authentically reflect the needs of young people. Incorporating youth culture encompasses everything from the way that materials are developed to the language used in training and outreach. By speaking to young people in their language, groups are able to engage marginalized youth in large numbers. For example, when youth organized against Proposition 21, youth organizations, community activists, and local hip-hop artists joined forces to organize hip-hop concerts to conduct mass political education. They also distributed flyers with youthful graffiti art that encouraged disenfranchised youth to vote and participate in the political process. A well-known Bay Area hip-hop artist and participant in the organizing effort commented, "Culturally, a lot of young people do not read newspapers or even if you pass them a flyer, they might read it but it's not as real to them because it's an old way of organizing. So hip-hop can bring us new tools to organize people with."[17]

How SJYD outcomes are different from other youth development approaches

SJYD yields a qualitatively different set of outcomes than does traditional youth development. First, it is more explicit about the serious social problems and conditions young people face. Second, it develops youth by seeing them not only as assets but also as agents capable of transforming their toxic environments, not simply developing resiliency and resistance to them. Third, SJYD fosters activism, civic engagement, and critically conscious citizens, the cornerstones of true democracy. In interviews with practitioners and researchers, Nat Williams, a researcher and program officer of the Hazen Foundation, accurately stated that if a young person "is doing well in school, has good parental support and mentored relationships, has positive self-esteem, contributes to others through service, but does not have an understanding of socio-political realities and how they affect him/her and their communities and is not working with others to challenge injustice in his/her or other environments, they may be great young people, but they are not fully developed."[18] This is particularly the case in a democratic society where consistent, informed, and active engagement in the civic process exemplifies good citizens. Prosocial youth development is important but not enough. Williams encourages researchers and practitioners to revisit their notions of healthy and full development.

More than any other intervention, SJYD fosters critical consciousness among youth who have been failed by other social supports, including traditional youth development programming. Critical consciousness can be described as an awareness of how institutional, historical, and systemic forces limit and promote opportunities for particular groups that lead to collective action to change unjust social conditions.[19] The development of critical consciousness includes a host of principles enumerated in traditional youth development frameworks, such as physical and psychological safety and security, emotional and moral support, and support-ive adult relationships.[20] SJYD goes further by supporting specific sociopolitical competencies.

- *Sociopolitical development and analysis.* Sociopolitical develop-ment emphasizes an understanding of the cultural, economic, social, and political forces that influence one's life. This under-standing shapes young people's worldview about systemic and root causes of social and community problems and requires that they act to change social conditions.
- *Social and community problem solving.* This refers to the capac-ity to collectively articulate social and community problems, as well as develop thoughtful and practical solutions. Often, this type of problem solving requires critical thinking about innovative strate-gies that have an impact on the quality of life for youth and their families.
- *Decision making.* A key component of healthy adolescent devel-opment is learning to be a good decision maker. SJYD organiza-tions support youth in becoming good decision makers by giving them the responsibility for deciding what needs to be done, how, and by whom. Youth are put in a context where they are supported in making decisions and seeing the impact of their decisions on themselves and their communities.
- *Healing and spiritual development.* One of the most devas-tating impacts of oppression is self-blame and hopelessness. However, critical consciousness allows young people who feel victimized to remove self-blame and heal from the trauma of poverty, racism, sexism, homophobia, and other forms of oppression. Healing can be described as psychological, emo-tional, and physical wellness. The healing process also leads to a spiritual development that provides youth with a sense of life purpose, empathy for the suffering of others, and optimism about social change.
- *Community well-being and just institutional practices.* SJYD out-comes focus on individual development, but there are social out-comes as well. When youth work to transform their environments,

the process and the result strengthen community well-being with the presence of safety, economic opportunities, and opportunities for recreation and productive civic engagement, the very conditions necessary to support the healthy development of individuals.

Even programs that do not have organizing for institutional change as an explicit goal can promote systems change. To determine whether they are doing so requires asking one basic question: How does the program help youth understand the root causes and the solutions to social problems? If a program is promoting a clearer understanding of root causes, it will facilitate long-term institutional change. Service programs can do much greater social good when they cultivate bonds of human solidarity and compassion and build critical consciousness. For many, the path of service leads from charity to justice. It is our job as SJYD practitioners to help clear that path and provide more resources for justice.

Increasing the investment in SJYD

The challenge to SJYD practitioners is to critically examine current practice and find ways to apply SJYD principles in efforts to support youth empowerment. When communities of practitioners have done so, as in the case of the Brazilian street children's movement, the results have been dramatic.[21] Fortunately, many organizations are creating paths for those committed to urban youth to follow. For funders and other allies seeking to promote the community change necessary to support authentic SJYD, the need for bold leadership is increasingly urgent.

For civil society to hold government accountable, it needs to be politically and financially independent. This means that SJYD needs strong support from private foundations and the broader community. Whoever is paying your bills often has the power to silence your voice. To ensure that young people can raise an independent voice for their own interests, we must increase the level of private philanthropic investment in SJYD.[22] One way to do this is to help see to it that 30 percent of all the funds going to youth development in the country be shifted to support SJYD as a key approach to working with marginalized youth. And beyond that, 10 percent of funding can go to support youth organizing as a core youth development strategy. There are many ways that funders can support SJYD. Following are some key recommendations:

- *Join existing SJYD funding collaboratives.* By joining the National Funder Collaborative on Youth Organizing or the California Fund for Youth Organizing, funders can make a responsible and effective contribution to supporting this new effort. Even if a foundation is starting a new SJYD or youth organizing funding initiative, commit within your own foundation at least 10 percent of your portfolio to an existing collaborative. Participating funders benefit tremendously from the learning relationships and knowledge already gained in these efforts.
- *Give larger grants to smaller organizations poised to grow.* Foundations like E. W. Hazen and Surdna have helped the field to grow by making substantial and smart investments in organizations with the potential to grow and make an impact. The field will be strengthened as other funders follow their lead.
- *Fund regional clusters.* Make a multiyear commitment to a region that is underresourced but strategically important, and fund multiple groups in that region. For SJYD practices to take hold, groups need close allies with whom they can share lessons and support.
- *Support regional intermediaries and capacity-building groups that are linked to regional clusters.* We must ask what organizational supports and opportunities SJYD initiatives and organizations need to develop and expand. There has been growth in the number of intermediary institutions working to support SJYD work in culturally and age-appropriate ways. These intermediaries are key to the development of youth organizing as a central SJYD strategy.[23] If there are no intermediaries in a region, look to partner with a national organization to build capacity into local groups for supporting SJYD over the long term.

• *Use a developmental framework for organizational and movement growth.* Youth development has helped us to look at young people in terms of the supports they need to navigate their stages of development successfully. We must bring this same approach to supporting the growth of groups and regional movements.

• *Involve practitioners in helping to identify organizations and distribute grants.* Philanthropy as a whole is recognizing the value of involving the people affected by an issue in distributing funds to organizations seeking to address that issue. In the SJYD field, this is of even greater importance.

Given the social, ecological, and political challenges that face our world today, the next generation cannot wait until they are adults to begin the work of building a more humane and sustainable world. In organizations around the country, young leaders are not just being taught about leadership; they are taking leadership and learning by doing—thus making organizations, schools, and communities more accountable, effective, and democratic. Given the low levels of participation in the formal political process demonstrated by adults, these forms of youth civic engagement are creating the next generations of civic leaders who will see voting not as the end of the political spectrum but as the beginning. Youth are strengthening democracy in America by building a more democratic political culture. It is time for the broader youth development community to lend its support and resources to this growing movement.

Notes

1. Irby, M., Ferber, T., & Pittman, K. (2001). *Youth action: Youth contributing to communities, communities supporting youth.* Takoma Park, MD: Forum for Youth Investment, International Youth Foundation; Pittman, J. K., & Cahill, M. (1991). *A new vision: Promoting youth development.* Washington, DC: Center for Youth Development and Policy Research Academy for Educational Development.

2. Garabarino, J. (1995). *Raising children in a socially toxic environment.* San Francisco: Jossey-Bass.

3. Brooks-Gunn, J., Ducan, G. J., Klebanov, P., & Sealand, N. (1997). Do neighborhoods influence child and adolescent development? *American Journal of Sociology, 99*(2), 353–395.

4. Ayman-Nolley, S., & Taira, L. L. (2000). Obsession with the dark side of adolescence: A decade of psychological studies. *Journal of Youth Studies, 3*(1), 35–48.

5. Males, M. (1996). *The scapegoat generation: America's war on adolescents.* Monroe, ME: Common Courage Press; Males, M. (1999). *Framing youth: Ten myths about the next generation.* Monroe, ME: Common Courage Press.

6. Message, W.I.T. (2001). *Soundbites and cellblocks; Analysis of the juvenile justice media debate and a case study of California's Proposition 21.* San Francisco: We Interrupt This Message.

7. Butts, J. (1999, October). *Youth violence: Perception versus reality.* Washington, DC: Urban Institute.

8. White, R. (1989). Making ends meet: Young people, work and the criminal economy. *Australian and New Zealand Journal of Criminology, 22,* 151–166.

9. Edin, K., & Lein, L. (1997). *Making ends meet: How single mothers survive welfare and low-wage work.* New York: Russell Sage Foundation.

10. Willis, P. (1977). *How working class kids get working class jobs.* Farnborough, UK: Saxon House.

11. Brooks-Gunn et al. (1997).

12. One example of increased criminalization within Proposition 21 was making $300 of property damage felony vandalism. This means that one ball through an expensive window could cost a youth a strike in a three-strikes system. Another example was Proposition 21's definition of a gang as three or more people wearing similar clothing. This broad description allows youth with no gang affiliation to be categorized as gang members and therefore subject to harsher penalties for the same crime than if they were not considered to be in a gang. For more on the details of Proposition 21, see www.lao.ca.gov/initiatives/2000/21_03_2000.html.

13. Irby et al. (2001); James, T. (1997). Empowerment through social change. *Bridges, 3*(4), 6–7; James, T., & Fernandez, R. (1998). It's all about power. *Third Force, 6*(1), 19–24; Mohamed, I., & Wheeler, W. (2001). *Broadening the bounds of youth development.* Chevy Chase, MD: Innovation Center for Community and Youth Development, and New York: Ford Foundation; Roach, C., Sullivan, L., & Wheeler, W. (1999). *Youth leadership for development: Civic activism as a component of youth development programming.* Chevy Chase, MD: Innovation Center for Community and Youth Development; Edwards, O., Johnson, N., McGillicuddy, K., & Sullivan, L. (2001). *An emerging model for working with youth: Community organizing + youth development = Youth organizing* (Occasional Paper). New York: Surdna Foundation.

14. Watts, R. J., Williams, N. C., & Jagers, R. J. (in press). Sociopolitical development and the making of African-American activists. *American Journal of Community Psychology.*

15. Ginwright, S., & Cammarota, J. (in press). New terrain in youth development: The promise of a social justice approach. *Social Justice.*

16. Local Initiative Support, Training, and Education Network (LISTEN Inc.) is a change agent that convenes, mobilizes, trains, and nurtures urban youth ages fourteen to twenty-nine to become leaders in transforming their communities. Based in Washington, DC, LISTEN Inc. was established in 1998 as a national capacity-building nonprofit organization to identify,

prepare, and support a new generation of leaders in poor urban communities of color. For more information, see www.lisn.org.

17. Sydell, L. (2000). Morning edition. National Public Radio; Hip Hop and Youth Organizing. Burrelle's Information Services, Box 7, Livingston, NJ 07039.

18. Interview with N. Williams, July 17, 2002.

19. Aspects of critical consciousness have been documented by organizations such as Leadership Excellence in Oakland California, which use identity development as a vehicle to political engagement.

20. Eccles, J., & Goodman, J. A. (Eds.). (2001). *Community programs to promote youth development.* Washington, DC: National Academy Press.

21. James, T., & McGuillicuddy, K. (2001). Building youth movements for community change. *Non-Profit Quarterly, 8*(4), 16–19.

22. Sullivan, L. (2002). *The state of youth organizing: 1990–2000: The state of philanthropy.* Washington, DC: National Committee for Responsive Philanthropy.

23. Resources range from the National Funders Collaborative on Youth Organizing, to long-time institutions like Youth Action, to newer intermediaries like LISTEN Inc. and the Movement Strategy Center. A directory can be found at www.movementstrategy.org.

SHAWN GINWRIGHT *is an assistant professor of sociology and ethnic studies at Santa Clara University and cofounder of Leadership Excellence in Oakland, California.*

TAJ JAMES *is executive director of the Movement Strategy Center, a national movement-building intermediary in Oakland, California.*

Youth conferences can be effective means for engaging youth in the life of their schools, communities, and nation, bringing benefits not only to youth themselves but also to the community, which gains through the energy, ideas, and values that youth contribute.

3

Youth conferences as a context for engagement

S. Mark Pancer, Linda Rose-Krasnor, Lisa D. Loiselle

WHEN YOUTH participate in decision making, they become engaged in the life of their communities. Meaningful youth engagement produces benefits to both youth and the community in which they live. Through engagement, youth gain a sense of empowerment

This research was funded by Health Canada through the Centre of Excellence for Youth Engagement, which focuses on effective strategies for engaging youth in making decisions for healthy living by providing support for youth in research, policy, and communications activities, as well as making the center itself a working model for youth engagement. For more on the Centre of Excellence for Youth Engagement, see www.tgmag.ca/centres/index.html. The opinions expressed in this chapter are the authors' and not necessarily those of Health Canada. We express our appreciation to the research team and others at Creating Change 2001: Maria Koumarelas, Maude Lamarre, Damien Alvarez-Toye, Leah Mae Francisco, Gisou Nourollahi, Stephanie Lajeunesse, Junior Therriault, Jean Paul Desjardins, Martin Latulippe, and Gabriela Pierre; to Rhonda Barron, Sarah Heger, and Zopito Marini for their assistance in data coding; and to Stoney McCart and the *New Directions* editors for their comments and suggestions on earlier versions of the chapter.

NEW DIRECTIONS FOR YOUTH DEVELOPMENT, NO. 96, WINTER 2002 © WILEY PERIODICALS, INC.

and form healthy connections to others, which are reflected in the reduction of risk behaviors and increases in positive activities by youth. In addition to the social benefits of these behavioral changes, the community gains through the energy, ideas, and values that youth bring to organizations, activities, and their relationships with adults. In this chapter, we provide a definition and conceptual framework for youth engagement, discuss some of the developmental outcomes associated with engagement, and describe how youth conferences can foster the engagement process.

Definition of youth engagement and conceptual framework

The active participation of community members is the cornerstone of any community development process.[1] It is through participation in program decision making that community members develop a sense of control or empowerment.[2] Community participation also fosters the development of improved programs and services[3] and a better match between the needs of the community and the kinds of services provided.[4]

Communities comprise individuals of all ages, including youth. Youth, like adults, benefit from participating in shaping the policies, programs, and environments that will affect their lives. The active and meaningful participation of youth in community life is just as important as the participation of adults, perhaps even more so, for it is at this stage in one's life that a sense of community and social responsibility is first formed.[5]

The key outcome of this kind of active participation is what Nakamura terms "vital engagement."[6] According to Nakamura, a youth can be vitally engaged in almost any sphere of activity, including music, politics, the arts, and community work. The key features of vital engagement in an activity are that the individual experiences "enjoyed absorption" in the activity that is sustained over time, the activity provides a link between the individual and the outside world, and the activity is felt to be meaningful and significant. Our own working definition of youth engagement is similar to that of Nakamura. We view engagement as the meaningful participation and sustained involvement of a young person in an activity that has a focus outside himself or herself. Full engagement consists of a behavioral component (such as spending time doing the activity), an affective component (for example, deriving pleasure from participating), and a cognitive component (for example, knowing about the activity). In the parlance of many youth organizations, this is parallel to a process described as "head, heart, feet" (Head: What did I learn today? Heart: How does it make me feel? Feet: What will I do? that is, next steps).

In attempting to understand how youth have become engaged or involved, we generated a conceptual model, based on research on youth volunteering by Pancer and Pratt[7] and a review of the literature on youth involvement. Our model delineates factors operating at two levels: individual and systems. According to the model, presented in Figure 3.1, youth initially become involved in an activity through the operation of various initiating factors. At the individual level, these factors may be things such as the influence of others—parents, friends, or teachers. At the systems level, an

Figure 3.1. Youth engagement framework

Individual Level

Teachers, friends	Supportive peer group	Community service	Enhanced self-esteem
Initiating Factors	Sustaining Factors	Participation, Engagement	Outcomes
Programs in community	Committees and boards with significant youth membership	Youth participation in decision making	More youth organizations

Systems Level

example of an initiating factor is the presence of youth-oriented organizations and activities in the community.

Youth engagement will be sustained only if, in addition to factors that initiate involvement, there are other sustaining factors present. At the individual level, engagement will be sustained if the youth has positive experiences within a supportive social milieu. At the systems level, engagement will be sustained if the youth is in an environment that has values, structures, and supports that promote youth engagement and sustain, encourage, reward, or permit the activities of adults who create the environment of youth engagement (for example, a school that encourages the active and meaningful participation of students in school governance).

If initiating and sustaining factors are present, then sustained and vital engagement will occur. This engagement can also be seen as occurring at two levels. At the individual level, engagement involves the individual's engaging in an activity on his or her own, such as providing community service or participating in a youth organization. At the systems level, the youth works in concert with others to affect an entire organization or system. An example of this kind of engagement would be youth members of a program committee who are working in partnership with adults to help organize community programs. Another example would be adult-youth partnerships to change the culture, processes, policies, and structures of organizations and systems to create youth-friendly environments that foster and sustain engagement.

Sustained engagement leads to the final element of our model, engagement outcomes, which can also occur at both an individual and a systems level. Examples of these outcomes are described in the following section.

Outcomes of youth engagement

At the individual level, the research literature indicates a host of outcomes associated with engagement, nearly all of them positive. One of the most commonly documented is a sense of self-esteem

and self-confidence, accompanied by an increased sense of competence and control.[8] Engagement is also associated with an increase
in personal and social skills,[9] a greater sense of direction in academic and career pursuits,[10] greater academic achievement,[11] and
a reduction in problem behaviors.[12]

Although the research literature tells us a great deal about individual outcomes associated with youth engagement or involvement,
it provides very little information about outcomes at the systems
level. One of the few comprehensive investigations of the impact
of youth involvement on systems is a recent study by Zeldin and
colleagues.[13] Their interviews with youth and adults from organizations with a strong reputation for involving youth in decision
making indicated that for many organizations, the organizational
culture changes as the principles and practices of youth involvement are adopted. The participation of young people helped clarify and focus the organizations' mission with regard to youth and
helped convince outside agencies, such as funding bodies, that the
organizations were serious about promoting the development of
youth. The organizations began to be more inclusive and repre-
sentative in their structure and were able to reach out to the community in more diverse ways.

Youth conferences

Given the strong evidence of positive outcomes associated with
youth engagement, how does one begin to foster engagement, particularly in communities where youth engagement is low and many
youth are experiencing considerable challenges? One potential
means is through youth conferences.[14] We describe the youth conferences conducted by the Students Commission, a national youth
organization operating in Canada, which bring together youth from
diverse backgrounds and geographical locations to express their
feelings about significant social issues, talk with other youth about
their own experiences, and develop policies, strategies, and programs that they can bring back to their communities to help better

the lives of youth. Conferences also bring youth into direct contact with government decision makers, allowing for an exchange of ideas and information that can benefit both youth and government.

The Students Commission, with offices in various parts of Canada, is a nonprofit organization, cofounded in 1991 by Tiny Giant Magazine, Optimist Clubs, and youth to organize annual youth-driven conferences. Organized for youth by youth in partnership with adults, the conferences provide an opportunity for young people from across Canada to come together and discuss social, environmental, and economic issues, prepare a national report, and present this report to government representatives and business, education, community, and labor leaders. The conferences also enable young people to take action in their own communities by providing them with the tools and resources to implement their recommendations. As a result, the conferences give youth a voice and allow them to mobilize action at the government and community levels.[15] Support for the delegates and their projects is provided by the Students Commission and continues well beyond the conference itself.

Since it began in 1991, the Students Commission has sponsored from one to four national youth conferences a year. The 2001 conference, Creating Change 2001, was attended by 87 youth (33 males, 54 females) between the ages of fourteen and nineteen, with one delegate aged twenty-five (M = 16.64). Delegates represented all ten provinces across Canada and several Aboriginal tribes, including the Blood Reserve in Alberta. Although most of the delegates spoke English, 10 recognized French as their first language. In addition, there were 39 youth, twenty-five years old and under (17 males, 22 females), returning from previous years' conferences or referred by other youth organizations, who attended to learn new skills and function as conference facilitators, speakers, and staff. The total number of youth in attendance was 126.

As with previous conferences, youth chose the topic for Creating Change 2001. An on-line poll early in 2001 identified violence, education, and discrimination as the preferred themes. To encapsulate these concerns, organizers decided to make the theme the empowerment of young people to create change with respect to all three issues. Creating Change 2001 lasted nine days, with three days of site and youth staff preparation prior to the arrival of delegates, five days of program activities, and one day of departure and wrap-up.

Youth were divided into nine working groups upon arrival at the conference. On each of the first three program days, delegates identified causes of violence, causes of discrimination, and problems within the education system. They also discussed possible solutions to the problems identified. These discussions led to the development of twelve national projects that could be carried out with the support of the Students Commission over the following year. Youth then signed on for one of the projects, and in project groups they created names and descriptions of their projects, mapped out their objectives, and developed action plans. On the final day of the conference, the project groups met with, and presented their ideas to, a variety of federal government officials and nongovernmental organizations.

Research and evaluation

Anecdotal evidence suggests that conferences such as Creating Change 2001 are successful in engaging youth; however, until this study, neither the program process nor its outcomes had ever been formally evaluated. The process component of our evaluation was designed to examine the aspects of the conference that made it successful, with the assumption that despite the changing topics of the annual conferences, there are critical processes of engaging youth that are consistent throughout the conferences each year. It is these processes, and not the specific topics themselves, that lead to desired positive impacts on delegates.

Because the core value of the Students Commission is to engage youth, young people were recruited to be involved in the data collection phase of the evaluation. Seven youth were assigned to the research team (three males, four females) in addition to four adult researchers (two males, two females). The research team also had an even representation of French- and English-speaking persons. The research group developed a multifaceted strategy for obtaining feedback from participants at the conference, which involved collection of the following data:

- Information about the conference process and events, consisting of field notes and videotapes of activities.
- Photographs of important conference activities taken by participants and research staff, with commentaries to be obtained by telephone interviews following the conference.
- Video interviews with conference participants focusing on conference expectations and experiences.
- "Letters to self," in which we asked participants (both delegates and staff) to tell us about their experiences and impressions of the conference. We received one hundred letters (sixty-three in English and six in French were included in our analysis; the rest declined to include their letters).

A narrative description of the conference process

One youth partner, in commenting on our rather academic definition of engagement, offered the following suggestion: "If you want to captivate me, tell me a personal story. Share with me an experience that changed your life in some way. When you're finished giving me a glimpse into this amazing moment of change, show me that this stuff you just told me about—getting involved, doing something that means something and accomplishing something awesome—is something that I can do too."

We have used field notes, interviews, and letters to self to generate a composite narrative account designed to provide a sense of what it is like to be a youth attending a first conference:

Imagine being sixteen years old and being asked to attend a conference that you don't know anything about. You leave your small hometown and fly halfway across Canada by yourself, to arrive at a large metropolitan airport. You wait nervously at the airport for someone that you have never met before to drive you thirty minutes to the conference site. You arrive in a town of approximately six hundred people and drive up to the entrance of the college where the conference will take place. You are one of eighty-six young people attending Creating Change 2001, a national youth-driven conference sponsored by the Students Commission. It's hard to decide how you are feeling: scared, nervous, shy, anxious, unsure. The next couple of hours are spent settling into your dorm room and getting to know your roommate for the week. You and your roommate wander around the campus together to orient yourselves. You come upon a group of delegates playing volleyball and join them. After an exhausting game, you all head over to the cafeteria for dinner.

Directly after dinner, everyone is asked to find their team leader and get into their team groups. The group facilitator starts off by having you introduce yourself along with a fruit you like to help people remember your name. The facilitator then asks everyone if they know why they are at the conference; nobody seems to really know. Your group is restless and distracted by other people milling around. After some discussion, your facilitator lets everyone go on their way and reminds you to return for the opening ceremonies at 8:30 P.M.

At 8:30, you enter a large gymnasium. Half of the gym is set up with a dozen round tables and chairs (one table for each team), a stage, and a glass booth near the back where the translators are waiting for the opening ceremonies to begin. You are given a lot of information. Staff talk about the expectations for the week, your role, rules, and several conference traditions. You play some games, and a few youth participate in improvisation on the stage.

It would seem that the night is almost over when the opening ceremony comes to a close; however, there is little sleep to be had this night. Your facilitator has asked you to be one of the panelists who will discuss a personal experience with violence tomorrow morning. Reluctantly you agree. You have never spoken in front of such a large group before, but you are up for the challenge. You stay up most of the night preparing and chatting with your roommate.

Over the next three days, you are expected to work from early morning to late in the evening, talking, planning, creating, and talking some more about three issues identified by youth as being important. Each of the next three days starts with an early-morning panel discussion. On the first program day, the theme is violence and its causes. The themes for the second and third days are discrimination and education and its problems. As a panelist this morning, you sit up on the stage with two other youth and talk about your experience with violence growing up in Iran and the fact that your father had been imprisoned. You are physically drained from a lack of sleep and emotionally drained as a result of your speech; nevertheless, you feel empowered because you were given an opportunity to share your experiences with others, and they listened to you with respect.

After a short break, you meet again with your group. Your task is to discuss further causes and types of violence. You start with an icebreaker to reintroduce yourselves and move on to the first question: causes of violence. After lunch, everyone assembles in the gymnasium again for the afternoon panel discussion: solutions to violence. Two new panelists talk about how they have personally dealt with the threat of violence. One young man discusses a plan he devised to reduce violence in his hometown. You are so intrigued that during question period, you ask for more information about the campaign, thinking that you can initiate a similar one in your hometown.

After the panel discussion, you again meet with your team group. This time your task is to identify solutions to violence. Your facilitator explains the idea of developing ideas for national projects that will later be presented to government officials for support. The facilitator wants the group to think of tools to design in the production room—creative ways of sending messages and sharing stories. Your group decides on promoting an antiviolence day. Your team will make drawings with sidewalk chalk, a video using themselves to share stories, and pamphlets and posters using pictures of the sidewalk chalk drawings. First, though, one person from your team must draft a summary of your discussions, which will go to the report room, where all of the information generated during the week will be put into a final report and distributed to everyone at week's end.

Dinner has come and gone, and your work for the day is not yet complete. Your team must regroup in the production room and create the tools (such as the video) discussed in the afternoon. A staff member shows your group how to operate the digital video camera. You find a deserted hall and rehearse your video. You spend the remainder of the evening filming and editing.

The next two days follow the same grueling pace. You talk at length about discrimination and problems within the education system. At the end of the third program day, an invitation has been extended to all delegates, facilitators, and staff to join a brainstorming session to create a list of potential national projects that will be developed further and presented to government officials in two days. You decide to attend the meeting. You find yourself in a room with twenty other people brainstorming ideas. You suggest the antiviolence day generated by your team. Your peers acknowledge this as a good idea, and it is put up on a flip chart. By the end of the meeting, eight or so pages of ideas have been generated. You will find out tomorrow which ideas will become national project topics after the conference organizers go through the list and decide which projects have enough potential to develop into something national.

The next morning, twelve flip charts are arrayed around the gymnasium, each displaying the title and a brief description of a project based on the ideas that came from the previous evening's brainstorming meeting. The organizers explain the twelve potential national projects, and then all the teams circulate around the room and visit each flip chart, where a staff member is standing by to provide more detail and take suggestions for improvement. Once everyone has had a chance to contribute ideas, you decide which national project you would like to work on during the coming year. You are delighted that the antiviolence day project your original team conceived will be one of the national projects and sign up for it. You meet briefly before lunch with your new national project team for introductions.

After lunch, the real work begins. You find yourself in the media room with eleven other youth interested in working on this project. Your facilitator explains what will happen the next day when you present the idea to the government. Your task as a group is to hammer out the details of the project. Later that afternoon, you are given the opportunity as a group to present your completed proposal to all the conference attendees. Some people work through the evening to put the final touches on their presentation. Your group will be presenting your Youth Against Violence Day campaign to the Crime Prevention Council.

Finally, presentation day has arrived. You quickly get up and put on your Students Commission T-shirt (given to everyone to wear at the presentation). On the bus, one of the staff members gives you a pep talk: your mission is to tell the government representatives about the project that you will be implementing over the next year. The goal of the meeting is to give the government an opportunity to be a part of your project and to collaborate with youth. You arrive in Ottawa, and your team describes your project to the Crime Prevention Council. Your presentation was good, and the government representatives were highly enthusiastic and said that the funding possibilities within their department next year were excellent. They also provided you with resources and contact information. It has been an awesome experience.

After such an exciting week, the rest of your day is spent doing some sightseeing and shopping in Ottawa. The conference ends with a banquet; a talent show featuring delegates, staff, and facilitators; dancing; and a long night of good-byes before the first delegates depart at dawn the next morning.

Letter-writing themes

Some major themes were expressed in the letters to self written by delegates and staff.at the conclusion of the conference:

• *Self-awareness and personal growth.* Many of the delegates indicated that they learned a lot about themselves from the conference. The process made them think and develop new points of view about the issues:

Nothing they [Students Commission} could have said could have prepared me for the actual conference. Someone told me as soon as I walked in that this would be a life-changing experience, and they couldn't have been more right.

• *Empowerment.* Delegates expressed the importance of getting to work on solutions and making a difference, as well as gaining specific skills, like speaking in front of a group:

It [the conference] gave us confidence to stand up to violence, discrimination, and education and voice our options, concerns, and experiences.

I learned that youth are the future, and we are the ones who can create change. We could all work together to make the world a better and safer place to live.

I'm excited about the fact that we actually got to speak to the government. We complain so much about how the government doesn't even listen, and here's a time when they actually did.

• *Awareness raising.* This category captured the delegates' learnings about the three conference topics (violence, discrimination, and education) and the diversity of related issues across Canada. Prior to the conference, many of the delegates had not been aware of the problems that youth outside their community face. A number of the delegates described how their increased awareness led directly to motivation to action:

I am going to try to not only educate myself but educate the people around me and people that I care about. Coming out of the meeting, I thought that this is my battle too.

I learned about the three topics we did and that Newfoundland seems pretty sheltered compared to other places in Canada. I mean, we all have our problems, but at our school, we don't have a lot of really bad violence or discrimination. And it seems as if across Canada, there are a lot of bad experiences for Aboriginals.

- *Hope for the future.* The most consistent hope was for implementation of the national projects that the delegates designed. Delegates also expressed hopes to attend future conferences and see new friends again:

I can't wait to see our team project get underway. I know it's gonna be so much work! But, ya know what? It's kinda exciting. This could go in history, and WE would be part of it.

- *Social relations: Fun and friendship.* This social category focuses on fun and friendship, the aspect of the conference that was probably the most frequently commented on. The delegates were happy with the opportunity to meet new people and make new friends. Some expressed initial anxiety about coming to the conference without knowing anyone, but most found friends quickly:

Throughout the days, we got closer and closer with each other. We were almost family. We became more outgoing and expressed our feelings in groups.

At first, I was so scared and nervous that I wasn't going to meet anyone and that I would be the outcast, but it turned out that I found many people who became my friends in a day.

- *Social relations: Values and beliefs bringing people together.* In this category, we tried to capture comments about the importance of the values and beliefs that people brought together. Some delegates expressed the importance of finding other people who shared their views, others identified the importance of hearing different views, and some delegates expressed both sides of this issue:

I've never been in that kind of atmosphere before where I was surrounded by people who are so diverse yet all have the same goal: to have their voice heard, to make a difference.

It was great to know that other students believe in the exact same thing as you. Also that they are willing to work just as hard as you to make a difference in the world.

At times, though, delegates found the group dynamics and diversity of viewpoints disconcerting:

The problem and frustration I had was with the power issues in my group. It was very uneven, and I found that most people would talk and talk but never shut up and listen to each other!

Analysis and discussion

The composite narrative and the letter-writing themes generated from our data analysis confirmed and illustrated a number of aspects of our engagement model.

The conference provided an extremely supportive social milieu for the youth, with staff constantly emphasizing the four pillars of the conference: respect, listen, understand, and communicate. The tasks and activities, undertaken as a team with an experienced facilitator as a guide, reinforced the feeling of support and at the same time provided youth with a sense of accomplishment. Other aspects of the conference, such as being listened to respectfully by their peers and by government and nongovernmental officials and seeing programs and policies that they themselves had created being considered for adoption, further enhanced the youth's experiences. These sustaining factors—a supportive social milieu combined with positive experiences—produced many of the outcomes, such as a feeling of empowerment and hope for the future, that youth described in their interviews and letters.

One of the key challenges for conference organizers is how to maintain the support that youth received during the conference after they return to their home communities. Organizers attempt to do this through a national e-mail bulletin board for each of the project groups where group members can exchange ideas and information, but not everyone has access to computer facilities. At a systemic level, further work needs to be done tracking the influence the youths' meetings with government officials had on those officials and the influence these youth had in their home schools and community organizations. In addition, we are working to supplement our qualitative, process-oriented research with more quantitative, outcome-oriented research. Although qualitative methods are an excellent way to describe and understand what goes on at a youth conference, the use of standardized quantitative outcome measures in the context of a rigorous evaluation design is needed to help gauge the benefits that youth participants derive from attending conferences compared to youth who do not have such opportunities.

We also need to move beyond the kinds of conferences organized by the Students Commission and examine other conferences and gatherings of youth in other settings to be able to identify the key elements that are necessary to produce optimal outcomes. These elements are likely to differ depending on the culture in which the conference is situated. What works in a Canadian context, for example, may differ substantially from what works in the United States or countries with even greater differences in their political structures, religious and cultural institutions, and mix of ethnicities.

The major themes generated from the letters align with the Students Commission's stated objectives, purposes, and expected outcomes for the conference and point toward the key ingredients for effective youth engagement processes and environments. These findings are supported by other work being conducted by the Centre of Excellence for Youth Engagement, including a scan of seventy-eight other youth organizations, the summary of which is just being released.[16]

The research literature tells us that youth participation can have a profound impact on almost every aspect of a youth's development. It can also produce significant change in the organizations and environments in which youth live, learn, work, and play. Youth conferences in which youth from different backgrounds are brought together to talk about solutions to social problems that affect their own lives promise to engage youth in ways that enhance self-awareness and personal growth, promote empowerment, raise awareness, make them feel respected and supported, and give them hope for the future. These kinds of conferences also have the potential to create change at the systems level, with youth learning how to create programs that will engage other youth in improving their schools and communities.

Notes

1. McNeely, J. (1999). Community building. *Journal of Community Psychology, 27*, 741–750.

2. Prestby, J., Wandersman, A., Florin, P., Rich, R., & Chavis, D. (1990). Benefits, costs, incentive management and participation in volunteer organizations: A means to understanding and promoting empowerment. *American Journal of Community Psychology, 18*, 117–150; Zimmerman, M. A., & Rappaport, J. (1988). Citizen participation, perceived control, and empowerment. *American Journal of Community Psychology, 16*, 251–278.

3. See, for example, Comer, J. P. (1976). Improving the quality and continuity of relationships in two inner-city schools. *Journal of the American Academy of Child Psychiatry, 15*, 535–545; Comer, J. P. (1980). *School power: Implications of an intervention project.* New York: Free Press; Hodgson, A. (1984). Efficient and effective human services: Some assumptions about why and how to involve community residents. *Canadian Journal of Community Mental Health, 3*, 27–38; Pancer, S. M., & Nelson, G. (1990). Community-based approaches to health promotion: Guidelines for community mobilization. *International Quarterly of Community Health Education, 10*, 91–111.

4. Iscoe, I. (1974). Community psychology and the competent community. *American Psychologist, 29*, 607–613.

5. Pancer, S. M., & Pratt, M. W. (1999). Social and family determinants of community service involvement in Canadian youth. In M. Yates & J. Youniss (Eds.), *Community service and civic engagement in youth: International perspectives* (pp. 32–55). Cambridge: Cambridge University Press; Youniss, J., & Yates, M. (1997). *Community service and social responsibility in youth.* Chicago: University of Chicago Press.

6. Nakamura, J. (2001). The nature of vital engagement in adulthood. In M. Michaelson & J. Nakamura (Eds.), *Supportive frameworks for youth engagement* (pp. 5–18). New Directions for Child and Adolescent Development, no. 93. San Francisco: Jossey-Bass.

7. Pancer & Pratt (1999).

8. Holland, A., & Andre, T. (1987). Participation in extracurricular activities in secondary school: What is known, what needs to be known? *Review of Educational Research, 57,* 437–466; Johnson, M. K., Beebe, T., Mortimer, J. T., & Snyder, M. (1998). Volunteerism in adolescence: A process perspective. *Journal of Research on Adolescence, 8,* 309–332; Lewis, B. A. (1991). Today's kids care about social action. *Educational Leadership, 49,* 47–49; Magen, Z., Birenbaum, M., & Ilovich, T. (1992). Adolescents from disadvantaged neighborhoods: Personal characteristics as related to volunteer involvement. *International Journal for the Advancement of Counselling, 15,* 47–59; Primavera, J. (1999). The unintended consequences of volunteerism: Positive outcomes for those who serve. *Journal of Prevention and Intervention in the Community, 18,* 125–140; Roker, D., Player, K., & Coleman, J. (1998). Challenging the image: The involvement of young people with disabilities in volunteering and campaigning. *Disability and Society, 13,* 725–741.

9. Lewis (1991); Roker et al. (1998).

10. Holland & Andre (1987); Johnson et al. (1998); Primavera (1999); Taylor, T., & Pancer, S. M. (2002). *Community service experiences and long-term commitment to volunteering.* Manuscript submitted for publication.

11. Eccles, J. S., & Barber, B. L. (1999). Student council, volunteering, basketball, or marching band: What kind of extracurricular involvement matters? *Journal of Adolescent Research, 14,* 10–43; Holland & Andre (1987); Markus, G. B., Howard, J.P.F., and King, D. C. (1993). Integrating community service and classroom instruction enhances learning: Results from an experiment. *Educational Evaluation and Policy Analysis, 15,* 410–419.

12. Eccles & Barber (1999); Youniss, J., Yates, M., & Su, Y. (1997). Social integration: Community service and marijuana use in high school seniors. *Journal of Adolescent Research, 12,* 245–262.

13. Zeldin, S., McDaniel, A. K., Topitzes, D., & Calvert, M. (2000). *Youth in decision-making: A study of the impacts of youth on adults and organizations.* Chevy Chase, MD: National 4-H Council.

14. Murray, C. (2002). *The impact of the Students Commission's National Youth Conference: A youth perspective.* Paper presented at the biennial meeting of the Society for Research on Adolescence, New Orleans; Pancer, S. M., Rose-Krasnor, L., Taylor, T., & Loiselle, L. (2002, April). *Getting youth engaged and involved: An evaluation of the Students Commission National Youth Conference.* Paper presented at the biennial meeting of the Society for Research on Adolescence, New Orleans.

15. Students Commission. (n.d.). About the Students Commission. Available on-line: www.tgmag.ca.

16. See www.tgmag.ca/centres.

S. MARK PANCER *is a professor in the Department of Psychology at Wilfrid Laurier University, Waterloo, Ontario, Canada, and a lead researcher with the Centre of Excellence for Youth Engagement.*

LINDA ROSE-KRASNOR *is a professor in the Department of Psychology at Brock University, St. Catharines, Ontario, Canada, and a lead researcher with the Centre of Excellence for Youth Engagement.*

LISA D. LOISELLE *is the coordinator of evaluation research for the Centre of Excellence for Youth Engagement and is based in the Psychology Department at Wilfrid Laurier University.*

Foundations are awakening to the untapped poten-
tial of serious, policy-focused community change
efforts led by teenagers and young adults. This
chapter lays out background questions, a point of
view, and programmatic strategies that one foun-
dation developed for supporting young people who
are taking direct action to improve their lives and
communities.

4

Building young people's public lives: One foundation's strategy

Robert F. Sherman

Prohibited from speaking as moral and political agents, youth become an empty category inhabited by the desires, fantasies, and interests of the adult world. This is not to suggest that youth don't speak; they are simply restricted from speaking in those spheres where public conversation shapes social policy and refused the power to make knowledge consequential with respect to their own individual and collective needs.[1]

Q. What gives you inspiration? A. I didn't think I had enough skills to join the fight. . . . One of the cement plants decided not to come because we did everything we can to stop them, so after that I felt I had enough faith to do anything. Also, a lot of my family and friends have asthma. Many people think it's caused by the area that we live in. Since it's in our community, I feel we must do something about it.[2]

NEW DIRECTIONS FOR YOUTH DEVELOPMENT, NO. 96, WINTER 2002 © WILEY PERIODICALS, INC.

"HEY THERE, student, teenager, young adult. Can we talk for a few minutes? I want to know about your *public life*, not your private life! What groups do you consider yourself part of? What is important to you in your community? What do you really care about? What bugs you about your school or your neighborhood? What is missing in your neighborhood that would help you grow up more involved, more concerned?"

Asking these questions about identity and how life might be improved—questions that get at the political intentions and social conditions lurking behind what young people feel and believe—sometimes fires the starter's gun in a process through which personal goals find expression in collective action to achieve desired community change.

When a young person begins to answer, another set of queries quickly rises up to complicate matters: "Who shares my same goals for change, and where can I find these folks? What can we *really* accomplish, just a few individuals, and young ones, at that? Haven't these problems—discrimination, poor education, disproportionate incarceration of juveniles and people of color, environmental degradation—been building for centuries? Who will teach us what to do? How long will it take? And centrally, whose role is it to make such changes? Aren't there 'experts' who know best? Isn't this what government is supposed to do for us, why we pay taxes?"

One foundation's response

This chapter takes up these questions, which are rarely asked, and describes a point of view and funding strategy developed by one foundation program, Effective Citizenry at the Surdna Foundation.[3] Effective Citizenry supports nonprofits that help young people work to achieve concrete community change on serious public problems consistent with their interests, group identities, and intentions. Its funding brings together teenagers and young adults, frequently with adults as allies, to tackle thorny public problems. Young people become conscious of their own potential as civic actors through their connections to community-based organizations that catalyze collective efforts to improve neighborhoods, institutions, and lives.

Because this work inevitably requires resources, connections, and colleagues, foundations have a chance to play supportive roles as partners in youth-directed community change.

A conundrum

No single angle of vision adequately captures how complicated and confounding young people today in fact are. Contradictions abound. In one public poll after another, teenagers and young adults express a wholesale repudiation of government and a vilification of public servants.[4] They do not believe politicians speak to them or care about their interests, a point made persuasively in Meredith Bagby's popular book *We've Got Issues.*[5] Still, young people feel deeply about their communities. They volunteer in record-high numbers (some estimate over 50 percent of them serve actively). Research shows repeatedly that they believe local work accomplished with their own hands is more important than political action or working for a cause.[6]

Similarly, young people today understand in their bones that they are a highly prized target market for corporate America's products. Yet, disappointingly to many observers, they fail to see themselves as a powerful collective force for community or social change.[7] Only a small number of teenagers and young adults choose organizing or other forms of group action to promote self-interest or mutually desired community improvement.

What do you really care about?

Before getting to the bones of Surdna's Effective Citizenry framework, consider one compelling grant outcome. (All projects described are past or current grantees in the Effective Citizenry program.) A San Francisco youth leadership program, Peer Resources, run by the San Francisco Education Fund, approached Surdna in 1998 citing persistent frustration among its students that their program taught the skills of *communicating* information to their peers about serious adolescent challenges (sexuality, violence, conflict), but did not help them *take action* to make changes closer to the causes of these problems. What could they do now other than talking and educating?

Forward-thinking program leaders sought to expand Peer Resources from peer leadership to youth organizing. Following some basic skill building, several young participants from various middle and high schools sat together to brainstorm and prioritize what troubled them and what they specifically wanted to change about their school experience. They discovered that each of them and people they knew felt personally victimized by constant sexual harassment at school, creating a painful ongoing situation with no obvious recourse or remedy. Attempts to meet with their school principals to explore the issue were repeatedly thwarted. When a meeting finally did take place, little emerged other than clarification that one high school's policy was to "tell the boy not to do it again." The students were angered and alarmed. Thus began a ten-month process that involved these actions:

1. Developing a survey instrument to poll more than four hundred high school peers in the district. Shockingly, 50 percent reported unwelcome physical contact, often five to ten times per day, and 65 percent reported sexual harassment during class. Few students had any awareness of district policy or remedy.
2. Based on the survey, forcing a set of meetings first with their school principals and then with other district leaders.
3. Organizing a larger group of students committed to improving San Francisco's policies and informing the media.
4. Researching sexual harassment policies in other jurisdictions.
5. Writing a booklet discussing sexual harassment in ways students would understand.
6. Proposing specific policy changes to the central board of education in San Francisco.

Not surprisingly, everyone was uncomfortable at some point in this process. (Democracy is messy.) Peer Resources staff, who operate programs in schools at the invitation of principals, were threatened with expulsion at several sites. One student was suspended, and others were afraid of negative impacts on their academic careers. Yet the young people persevered, taking strength from one another and their optimism that progress could be made.

The story has a happy ending. Within one year, new policies were adopted by the adult leadership of the San Francisco Board of Education, including "must-report" procedures, mandatory staff training, and a prominent place for the issue in all student handbooks. What began as a discussion of common experiences and shared pain resulted in benefit for the entire student population in San Francisco. The process involved no make-work for students or a make-believe outcome for their district. Young people took the reins and helped craft policy by assuming advocacy roles normally reserved for, or tightly guarded by, adults.

Direct action to solve serious community problems

Early experiences with organizations whose work unleashed nascent, untapped civic activism led by young people themselves encouraged changes within Surdna's Effective Citizenry program. One overall intention has been our guidestar: to support young people as they take direct action to solve serious problems in their schools, neighborhoods, and the larger society. As the foundation began considering new funding priorities and guidelines in 1999, four categories of questions emerged:

• How do we view young people: as problems to be fixed (teenage moms, drug addicts, politically disengaged, dropouts) or as community assets—full participants in community life, shapers of their own development, potential agents of social change, institution builders? What have we learned from recent youth development theory, research, and promising practice on these dimensions?

• Are teenagers and other young people in training waiting to become effective civic actors at some still-to-be-determined time in the future? Or can they become capable now of taking on serious, collective public work in order to fix their institutions and communities?

• Can we resolve contradictory views of young people as disengaged from conventional politics yet deeply concerned about and committed to their communities?

• What values must underlie our grant-making choices?

As we wrestled with these questions, the research, and our own experience in youth and community development, we became increasingly convinced of three things. First, community-based efforts through which teenagers and young adults together tackle serious public problems help young people grow up aware of their own civic potential and of the hard work it takes to make change. Second, armed with specific skills for democratic participation and connected to organizations that provide allies and a platform for collective work, young people have a chance to firm up their identities as effective participants in community life. And finally, communities are improved and strengthened by the direct work and vitality of engaged, skilled youth.[8]

Seeking to keep our framework and guidelines simple, we identified two core strands for funding: (1) young people (teenagers and young adults) taking direct action to address serious social problems and (2) building the infrastructure to make this activism as effective as possible. The two sides of our grant making are mutually reinforcing, leading to better outcomes for young people and communities and to a more solid field of practice.

Grants promoting direct action have clustered naturally into three areas: education reform (through which high school students are entering the policy and school financing fray swirling around urban school districts), justice reform (focused on redressing the current public prioritization of spending on prisons over education or other nonpunitive strategies), and youth-created media (aimed at reforming how the wider public views young people's interests and roles in communities). Effective Citizenry also funds school district-wide service-learning programs aimed at deepening students' connections to their communities supported by formal learning.

Strengthening the groundwork for these meaningful community change efforts by young people involves funding intermediary organizations that train, teach, and provide adult allies for youth-initiated direct action. Surdna is also interested in advancing theory, research, documentation of effective practice, and building networks. The importance of infrastructure cannot be understated. Without adequate organizations, funding, training, technical and management assistance, availability of allies, networks, evaluation strategies, documentation, and other supports, continued encouragement of deeper levels of youth civic engagement (well beyond community service) will stall.

Public is collective

Effective Citizenry did not arrive at its intentions alone. A raft of recent books and articles encourage robust democratic participation by local community members. Examples and analyses differ, but the prevailing idea is that people with public goals must emerge off the sidelines, renounce the expertise of policy wonks and the exclusive control of government officials, find allies, and take active roles as citizens in a democracy.[9] Authors restate the obvious: that no individual is alone in community. Public life, we read, is relational. Many others always share social and community circumstances, and we find one another through community institutions or associations.

As Lappe and duBois flesh out in *The Quickening of America*, each of us lives a public life, whether consciously or not.[10] Passive acceptance of the way things are, that is, doing nothing, is just as political a position as seeking to change conditions, behaviors, or policies. Lappe and duBois invite us to join the democratic tradition of deciding for ourselves who potential civic actors are. The burden is on all of us to upend major constraints on grassroots community stewardship.

Young people have public lives too

Many authors emphasize the collective nature of democratic participation in adult communities and even strain to see the outlines of a civic renewal movement,[11] and a growing number are focusing specifically on the civic energy being generated by and around young people. Boyte resuscitates the useful concept from the 1930s of public work and applies it to the talents, interests, and situations of young people today. He and coauthors write, "Public work is a framework for reinventing an active practice of citizenship. . . . [It] stresses practical public effort by ordinary people in everyday environments such as neighborhoods, schools, 4-H clubs, government agencies, nursing homes, religious congregations, community groups, service organizations, and other settings in helping to create and build—to 'produce' the world around us." The authors view a recent shift of focus from youth volunteerism (meeting human needs, usually individually) to youth civic engagement (examining community priorities, behavior, and policies, always in groups) as an emerging concept in the public discourse.[12]

A myriad of formal education strategies seek to build such civic competence and interest.[13] School-based programs, even ones tied to formal course work, can promote deeper levels of engagement and responsibility, as shown in another illustration from Surdna's grant portfolio. HOME Project (run by nonprofit Alternatives in Action) was initiated by the school district in Alameda, California, as an experiment: a possible antidote to high levels of student apathy, poor academic outcomes, and alarming dropout rates. HOME challenged its initial cadre of thirty teenagers to codesign their afternoon academic program, first, by identifying the opportunities and supports that a young person in Alameda would need in order to grow up healthy and involved, and second, by inventing a group process that would allow young people to create those assets. Of course, students and staff quickly discovered that the two developed in tandem, each reinforcing the other.

On the individual student level, HOME focused on taking risks and taking responsibility. They were encouraged, for example, to risk taking on an assignment, such as making a presentation at a city council meeting, and to be certain that they had done the necessary background work and developed the necessary skills (ideas, research, appreciation of audience, a plan with recommendations, public speaking ability). They also had to become responsible to the group for showing up and doing the best job possible. In fact, over time, HOME evolved a list of 5Rs: risk, responsibility, relationships, rigor, and real.

On the community improvement level, HOME members tackled real problems right away. The group's first major project was to build a giant skate-park for local teens, who at that time had few recreation options. They explored potential sites, developed plans, estimated costs, raised the funds from the public coffer by lobbying a resistant city council, identified the nine hundred adult allies who would volunteer to help construct the park, and so on. HOME next opened a teen employment center to place young people in good long- and short-term jobs (275 placed to date). Two years later, it located a building on a decommissioned naval base on the San Francisco Bay for its expanding needs (hundreds of youth have joined its after-school programs), secured a lease, and then renovated, involving 700 community volunteers.

And in 2001, HOME students applied for and secured the first-ever youth-written charter for a charter high school in California. Such ongoing and visible public work has positively affected the way teenagers are viewed in Alameda. (Preliminary evaluations have found some evidence of a positive shift of public attitudes toward young people. A more substantive evaluation is under way.) In seven years, they have made substantial progress for youth on matters of recreation, employment, and education. In each case, public funds and priorities were redirected toward young people and their institutions based on direct youth action.

Civic activism can be effective youth development

Most positive youth development frameworks posit that growth and change can occur simultaneously on three important dimensions when young people take a direct hand in their own development and work together toward policy or systems change.[14] At Surdna, we see these three levels as intertwined and mutually reinforcing.

First, *young people themselves develop and grow* when they become civic activists by mastering and applying an important set of skills: evaluating a serious public problem, understanding their own and others' relationship to that problem, researching issues in order to map the roles of players and their power relations, planning a response, and securing partners for the effort. Often, writing, public speaking, networking, and collaborating are hard skills on which young people make substantial progress when participating in institutional reform efforts.[15]

Next, *new institutional practices* are invented by organizations where young people lead, govern, and make decisions. A small literature is developing, for example, on the topic of youth governance and institutional transformation.[16]

Finally, *the community can be changed concretely* through organizing and public work: a new sexual harassment policy is put in place; a chemical plant is now monitored by regulatory authorities; a proposed curbside recycling program is finally instituted; the press extensively covers youth and community voices raised against building new juvenile prisons.[17]

The teenage and young adult years are the right time

All three levels of change—individual, institutional, community—are important to teenagers and young adults. Forging a solid identity, in the crucible of peer experience, is among the chief developmental tasks of these life periods. Intellectual and emotional attentiveness to broad social questions is fueled in many cases by idealism, a hunger for belonging, and a search for meaningful roles.[18] Young people are first concerned with growing up and establishing themselves. Second, they seek challenging roles in their community institutions. Finally, they want to see their worlds change for the better. Adolescent development theory suggests that no other group is better prepared than young people to understand intuitively our interconnectedness and the urgency of public problems.[19]

Moreover, these life periods offer the first opportunities to test out values through action. Passionate moral exploration comes with the territory. At Surdna, we see a short list of specific values evoked by young people over and over—fairness, equity, justice, and the importance of inclusion—that reprises America's most fundamental, democratic principles. Effective Citizenry's guidelines place these values front and center.

Now or later? Who can wait?

Most serious problems cannot wait for attention and action to be taken at some future date. And just as they are animated by peers and by values, young people feel the urgency to act once they know they can. Consider the example of Youth United for Community Action (YUCA) in East Palo Alto, California, the "poor" suburb of Stanford University's wealthy town. YUCA participants, usually fifteen teenagers working as a core group but attracting the involvement of scores more when necessary, have worked for five years to bring attention and regulatory sanction to the Romix Corporation, a toxic waste and computer chip recycling facility that has been operating since 1991 on an expired permit. A series of actions against Romix were conceived, researched, and carried out by YUCA members. Their organizing eventually secured a regulatory investigation leading to changes in Romix's practices. Young people have led close to two thousand community residents on "toxic tours" of the neighborhood, which raise community consciousness. The press has covered the issue steadily. With a polluter right at the doorstep, could YUCA's young people afford to wait until adults believed they were "ready" to take action on this environmental threat?

Failing and crumbling schools can also fuel passionate public responses. Youth organizers working on education reform in cities across the country have been dealing with concerns that are central to their development and futures: the adequacy of their education. Described in some detail in Chapter Five in this volume and also in earlier work,[20] students in Philadelphia have organized to challenge student passivity in the face of deteriorated buildings, poor instruction, stark disparities in the education available in different neighborhoods, state financing formulas and its discrimination against students in urban schools, youth–security officer relations, outdated curricula, and a host of other important topics.

Working initially through after-school clubs, the Philadelphia Student Union and Youth United for Change have now established chapters in close to a dozen high schools. Students have participated in policy and planning in very public, visible, and real ways. Youth organizers are not simply preparing, waiting for a moment when authority will be conferred on them. They are seizing a rightful place as community members directly affected by inadequate conditions now, providing a vehicle for student anger as well as policy development and proposed remedies.

Similarly, young people in several states, but particularly in California, have been challenging the criminal justice system (see Chapter Two, this volume). The rapid expansion of juvenile prisons across the country, statistical overrepresentation of black and brown youth and young adults in the criminal system, and national trends toward tougher sentencing laws have led to urgent responses by youth organizers. Framing issues for young people and the wider public as matters of public priority setting, as well as of human rights and social justice, has rallied youth across the country.

Media: Problem and solution

Although acceptance is building for the idea that young people can or should take on public problem-solving roles formerly reserved exclusively for adults, there is still a long way to go. Mainstream media's predominant representations of young people are fundamentally bleak. News and entertainment media hammer the public with steady messages, most backed up by no data whatsoever, that teenagers and young adults are disengaged from community life and put society at risk.[21] Their bodies are beautiful, but their interests are shallow. The generation is portrayed as materialistic and individualistic, with young people focusing more on individual rights and prosperity than on collective responsibilities. Furthermore, we learn repeatedly from the media, young people commit crimes and are incarcerated in alarming numbers.

Unhappily, some of these negative pronouncements hit the mark. We know that young people vote in record low numbers and therefore do not engage in even the most rudimentary form of democratic participation. Polls reveal that teenagers and young adults mistrust politicians and government more than any other generation in recent history.[22] Their civic knowledge (history, how government works, ways Americans participate at the grassroots) is woefully inadequate.[23] They barely consume news (a sign of disinterest in the wider world) when compared to earlier generations.

Interestingly, young people themselves are challenging endemic media frames through youth journalism and youth-led investigations of mainstream media bias. A burgeoning youth media movement presents the politically attuned voices of young people in print, on the radio and, importantly, in newly invented on-line forms such as zines and Web sites. Notably, in 2002, Youth Radio, a youth media program in Berkeley, California, which brings intelligent teen reportage and commentary to adult audiences on the radio, was recognized with a George Peabody Award for Excellence in Journalism, among the media's highest honors. LA Youth, a print journalism shop, fills two pages each month in the *Los Angeles Times*, a major mainstream newspaper.

And teenagers working through We INTERRUPT This Message, a media advocacy organization also in the Bay Area, have systematically challenged youth representation at three major media outlets (KTVU in San Francisco, the *San Francisco Examiner*, and the *New York Times*) to good effect. In 2001, analyzing the form and content of 257 stories about youth seen on KTVU news, INTERRUPT's Youth Media Council corroborated the findings of earlier studies: "Repeatedly, studies have shown that news coverage of youth gives the public a picture of race, poverty, education and crime that leads to increased spending on punishment as a policy solution for youth, economic policy that increases poverty, educational policy that decreases equality, and a criminal justice system that calls for harsher penalties and increased punishment for youth.

A clearer picture of youth is necessary to create effective public policy."[24] Young people themselves are crafting more nuanced and balanced representations.

Digital media are part of the everyday lives of youth. Internet interactivity, for example, encourages a creative interplay of personal interests, information, and resources developed elsewhere. Young people access this new medium to plan and organize around issues, explore policy innovations in other places, or seek out case histories of effective community change. Web sites such as www.YouthNoise.com, which aggregates content from scores of other Web sites and links youth to opportunities to learn and serve, become important tools in the mobilization and strategy sharing for young people.

Needed: Strong youth-led organizations

Media are not the only challenge. The general thrust of this chapter is that individual interests and goals for change achieve heft and power only when united with others through the work of organizations. Organizations, particularly vulnerable youth-led ones, need care and feeding in order to thrive. Youth leadership and governance of community nonprofits is fairly new, and skillful practice is only now being developed and documented. Greater foundation attention to intermediary organizations that improve effectiveness is critical.

Here are examples of important intermediary efforts. LISTEN Inc., based in Washington D.C., helps emerging youth-led community change efforts get off the ground. It consults to young staff members on a range of competencies: aligning mission and vision with resources and growth plans, board development, fundraising, and campaigns. LISTEN's consultations help youth-led groups strengthen areas of organizational weakness. Without such attention, many nascent efforts wither.

Other intermediaries offer more targeted consultation. The Data Center in Oakland, California, helps youth-led organizing groups learn deep research skills necessary to map out effective campaigns—for example, how to follow the money trail between politicians and corporations, investigate the health effects of a specific pollutant, or understand demographic changes. The John W. Gardner Center for Youth and Their Communities, headquartered at Stanford University, helps train young people in schools and community-based organizations in ways to map their community's resources available to young people, helping them become active in local policy development aimed at amplifying opportunities and redressing disparities.

Another important example of infrastructure support is found in the Funders Collaborative on Youth Organizing. The collaborative, comprising national, regional, and local foundations as well as practitioners, works to substantially increase philanthropic investment in youth organizing across the country[25] in a number of ways:

- Making direct grants ($1.2 million regranted to date)
- Giving large foundations access to grassroots efforts otherwise too small to consider
- Establishing learning networks for youth organizers and intermediary organizations
- Broadening the range of good technical assistance providers
- Encouraging evaluation and documentation of youth organizing

Involvement with the Funders Collaborative on Youth Organizing meets many of Surdna's goals: finding foundation partners and amplifying available resources, improving the work on the ground in a substantial number of places, and building an evidence base on the effectiveness of youth organizing that can be widely shared.

Deeper levels of participation

It is encouraging that twenty-six foundation partners now actively participate in the Funders Collaborative on Youth Organizing and that other forms of youth civic engagement are beginning to find greater levels of financial support within American philanthropy. But just as the images of young people in the media are tough to challenge and slow to advance, changing foundations' interests and evolving programmatic responses continues to be a serious challenge.

In the two years since Effective Citizenry adopted its tight focus on the deeper levels of youth participation in improving institutions and communities, we have learned that the work is tough, not always successful (it is real, after all), long term, both sloughing and exciting. Certain hallmark characteristics are invariably found:

- A focus on a specific, persistent social problem that affects many in the community and not just individuals.
- A coming together of like-intentioned youth who want to compel substantial change on that community problem.
- Young people working through an organization. Isolated, individual efforts or volunteering do not fit here.
- Study and analysis of the problem and proposed remedies: historical and current background, analysis of power dynamics, and identification of the potential levers of change. Efforts always seek to influence key players, (frequently government, corporations) and change conditions or policies.
- Leadership of young people themselves for these collective enterprises through formal governance roles. Adult allies and staff of organizations provide access, guidance, and partnership.

So go ahead, ask the questions

"So, hey, young person, let's agree to ask and pursue the questions posed at the beginning of the chapter everywhere we might get answers. And hey, adults, take on new, collaborative roles with young people as they build effective public lives right now. We can't afford to whisper or to wait. The stakes for this country's citizens, young and old, are as high as the needs of our communities and schools are deep."

Notes:

1. Epstein, J. (Ed.). *Youth culture: Identity in a postmodern world.* Cambridge, MA: Blackwell, 1998.

2. White, S. (2002, May). Young activists work for a brighter day: East Palo Alto. *YO! Youth Outlook!,* p. 7.

3. The Surdna Foundation in New York City is a family philanthropy established in 1917 by John E. Andrus. Formal guidelines can be found at www.surdna.org.

4. Is anyone listening? (2002, Spring). *Trust Matters: An Issue Report from the Partnership for Trust in Government,* no. 1; two public opinion surveys for Public Allies by Peter Hart Research, 1998, 2002.

5. Bagby, M. (2000). *We've got issues: The get real, no B.S., guilt-free guide to what really matters.* New York: Public Affairs Books.

6. Is Anyone Listening? (2002, Spring).

7. Craig, M., & Raj, R. (2002, July 12). *Marketing and young people: An overview.* Paper presented at a meeting sponsored by the Pew Charitable Trusts, Philadelphia.

8. Cornerstone Consulting Group. (2001). *Communities and youth development: Coming together.* Houston: Author.

9. Good references are: Schultz, J. (2002). *The democracy owners' manual: A practical guide to changing the world.* New Brunswick, NJ: Rutgers University Press; Lappe, F., & and duBois, P. (1994). *The quickening of America: Rebuilding our nation, remaking our lives.* San Francisco: Jossey-Bass; Sirianni, C., & Friedland, L. (2001). *Civic innovation in America: Community empowerment, public policy, and the movement for civic renewal.* Berkeley: University of California Press.

10. Lappe & duBois (1994).

11. Sirianni & Friedland (2001); Loeb, P. (1999). *Soul of a citizen: Living with conviction in a cynical time.* New York: St. Martin's Press.

12. Skelton, N., Boyte, H., & Leonard, L. (2002). *Youth civic engagement: Reflections on an emerging public idea.* Minneapolis: Center for Democracy and Citizenship, University of Minnesota.

13. Gibson, C. (2001). *From inspiration to participation: A review of perspectives on youth civic engagement.* Berkeley, CA: Grantmaker Forum on Community and National Service; Cutler, D. (2002). *Taking the initiative: Promoting young people's involvement in public decision-making in the USA.* London: Carnegie Young People Initiative, UK; Westheimer, J., & Kahne, J. (2002, August). *What kind of citizen? The politics of educating for democracy.* Paper presented at the annual meeting of the American Political Science Association, Boston.

14. See the extensive writings of Karen Pittman, James Connell, Milbrey McLaughlin, publications of the Search Institute, and Public/Private Ventures. For a youth development field overview, see Benson, P., & Pittman, K. (Eds.). (2001). *Trends in youth development: Visions, realities and challenges.* Norwell, MA: Kluwer.

15. Sullivan, L. (2000, February). *An emerging model for working with youth: Community organizing + youth development = Youth organizing.* New York: Surdna Foundation.

16. Zeldin, S., McDaniel, A., Topitzes, D., & Calvert, M. (2001). *Youth in decision-making: A study on the impacts of youth on adults and organizations.* Chevy Chase, MD: National 4-H Council.

17. Irby, M., Ferber, T., & Pittman, K., with Tolman, J., & Yohalem, N. (2001). *Youth action: Youth contributing to communities, communities supporting youth.* Takoma Park, MD: Forum for Youth Investment, International Youth Foundation.

18. Kipke, M. (Ed.). (1999). *Risks and opportunities: Synthesis of studies on adolescents.* Washington, DC: National Academy Press.

19. Erikson, E. (1963). *Childhood and society.* New York: Norton; Piaget, J. (1977). *The essential Piaget* (H. Gruber, Ed.). New York: Basic Books.

20. Cervone, B. (2002, Spring). *Fires in the bathroom: Advice from kids on the front lines of high school.* Providence, RI: What Kids Can Do.

21. Amundson, D., Lichter, L., & Lichter, S. (2001). *What's the matter with kids today: Television coverage of adolescents in America.* Washington, DC: FrameWorks Institute.

22. Center for Information and Research on Civic Learning and Engagement. (2002, March). *The political and civic engagement of young adults in America.* Washington, DC: Lake, Snell, Perry & Associates.

23. Fletcher, M. (2002, July 4). Struggling to get civics back into the classroom. *Washington Post,* p. 1; Gibson (2001), p. 5.

24. Youth Media Council. (2002). *Speaking for ourselves: A youth assessment of local news coverage.* San Francisco: We Interrupt This Message.

25. From the collaborative: "We define youth organizing as a comprehensive youth development and social justice strategy that trains young people in community organizing and advocacy, and assists them in employing these skills to alter power relations and create meaningful institutional change in their communities. Youth organizing relies on the power and leadership of youth acting on issues defined by and affecting young people and their communities, and involves them in the design, implementation and evaluation of these efforts."

ROBERT F. SHERMAN *is program director for Effective Citizenry at the Surdna Foundation, New York City.*

*The experiences of urban public high school stu-
dents, told in their own words, offer new and vet-
eran teachers guidance on how to reach adolescent
learners and illustrate what youth-adult partnerships in the classroom might look like.*

5

Moving youth participation into the classroom: Students as allies

Barbara Cervone, Kathleen Cushman

MORE THAN twenty-five years ago, the National Commission on
Resources for Youth argued that youth can contribute meaningfully to their communities and, in the process, to their own development. "What they cannot do on their own," the commission
concluded, "is create the climate and the conditions that will permit them to take these participatory roles in society on a wide-
spread scale. That is the challenge and the task of the adult
world."[1]

Creating such a climate and conditions remains our challenge, perhaps most of all in urban high schools, where the language of youth-
adult partnerships sounds downright foreign. The voices of high
school students shared here offer some much-needed translations.

For more about What Kids Can Do, see www.whatkidscando.org. For a rich array
of ideas, publications, and resources on youth development and the promise of
youth participation, see www.theinnovationcenter.org, www.atthetable.org, and
www.forumforyouthinvestment.org.

NEW DIRECTIONS FOR YOUTH DEVELOPMENT, NO. 96, WINTER 2002 © WILEY PERIODICALS, INC.

When everyone wins

Books Not Bars is the first time I've had something so important to participate in. I now know more than most kids at my school—about how the education and juvenile justice systems connect, about how to analyze a speaker or writer's perspective, about how to motivate people. It makes me want to run something myself! [Alan, age fourteen, San Francisco]

In 1996, a group of youth and adults seasoned in the field of youth development laid the foundation for a national movement for youth participation. They imagined a society in which youth helped to make the decisions that affect them. "Youth want to participate, and more adults are realizing [that] the long tradition of making decisions for youth without youth [has] failed," said one youth advocate.[2]

In the years since, the campaign for youth participation has become a mainstay of effective youth development practice. Indeed, a 1998 survey found that about half of all nonprofit organizations involved young people in decision-making and leadership roles.[3] "The time is right for a surge forward in America's investment in youth action."[4]

Like many other ideas that spread broadly, the term *youth participation* has come to wear multiple faces—civic engagement or activism, youth-adult partnerships, and youth governance, empowerment, or voice—and the distinctions can be important. Young people serving on nonprofit boards or advisory committees is quite different from youth and adults together campaigning for safer neighborhoods or against increased funding for jails instead of schools. Nontraditional youth leadership training builds different skills from those gained through youth programming on local public radio stations.

A growing body of research "footnotes the common sense," youth advocate Karen Pittman often says, that youth benefit when adults value their voices and actions. Resilience studies have long shown that successful youth development depends on relationships and opportunities to participate.[5] The links among youth identity, meaningful engagement, and positive youth development have proven extraordinarily powerful.[6] And research findings that our ability to work effectively with others develops most deeply in adolescence and young adulthood remind us of the urgency of promoting these links.[7]

Only recently, however, has attention turned to studying how youth participation affects the adults and organizations that serve young people. In a groundbreaking study, researchers at the University of Wisconsin–Madison found that after adults experienced firsthand the competency, vitality, and perspectives of youth, their own commitment, energy, and sense of mastery increased.[8] Young people also helped clarify an organization's mission. As one program director observed, "If you involve kids, they'll tell you what does and does not work right away." Everyone wins, youth and adults alike, when we prize the participation, ideas, and contributions of young people.

When we do not, we all lose. Where adolescence, poverty, and an absence of supports coincide, the negative outcomes for youth are all too familiar. Drugs, violence, social isolation, pregnancy, truancy, and academic failure, harbingers of dead-end futures, are their most visible indicators, showing up in newspaper headlines as well as years of scholarly research. Adults attempting to engage these youth, whom they view as unreachable, often feel like failures too, packing up their discouragement and moving on to work they view as more rewarding.

For many in the field of youth development, these findings and perspectives have coalesced into a set of related convictions. First, all young people, advantaged and not, need a blend of services, supports, and opportunities to thrive. Second, the notion that marginalized youth need to be "fixed" must give way to a commitment to development that motivates growth, change, and participation at every step. Third, youth in partnership with adults have crucial roles to play as stakeholders in the programs and institutions that affect them—most of all, in those pledged to their well-being. Adults and their organizations benefit as much as young people do when these partnerships thrive.[9] These principles seem curiously distant from the daily goings-on of most American high schools.

If you pay attention, you can see it

Don't just look at students for answers, but look at who we are, through the way we act. Not "what's going on in our home life"—be perceptive to what's going on in our classroom—Who we like, what's hard for us, what's easy for us. If you pay attention you can see it. [Vance, age eighteen, New York City]

In too many classrooms across the country, students like Vance speak of being barely visible, and too many teachers struggle just to get kids to show up, a symptom of a persistent divide, pitting teachers and students on seemingly opposing sides. In a 2001 national survey, for instance, 65 percent of students agreed with the statement, "My teachers don't understand me," and 33 percent of teachers reported inadequate preparation to reach students with backgrounds different from their own. (By comparison, only 4 percent felt underprepared to implement curriculum and performance standards.) In the previous year's survey, 39 percent of students said they trust their teachers "only a little or not at all."[10]

Certainly we see exceptions: dedicated teachers who routinely pay attention to students; purposeful projects that promote students as resources or creators of knowledge; small schools that every day put students at the center and where students speak of being deeply engaged in learning and of their teachers as family. But the one-way transmission of knowledge and skills from teachers to students remains the dominant paradigm in most classrooms, with test scores tallying how well both parties have done. Maintaining order is the undercurrent in most discussions about student-teacher relationships. And few of the prevailing theories about improving schools identify students as stakeholders or embrace meaningful student engagement as an input as well as an output.

If the principles of youth participation make sense in youth programs outside school, certainly they have a role inside the classroom. But this terrain is largely uncharted. How can these ideas move beyond the student councils, clubs, and extracurricular activities where they are traditionally sequestered and into daily classroom exchange? How can student voice breathe new meaning into the phrase *class participation* or transform student-teacher interactions into partnerships of mutual respect rather than skirmishes for control? And how can teachers break through the barriers of adolescent identity and culture to truly reach students, typically from backgrounds different from their own?

In the spring of 2002, Kathleen Cushman, a writer with the organization What Kids Can Do, with support from MetLife Foundation, worked with forty high school students—almost all of color, half of them recent immigrants, from four U.S. cities—to plumb their classroom experiences for answers to these questions.[11] In a series of intensive writing and interview sessions totaling more than seventy-five hours and 100,000 words, the students spoke and wrote about their daily encounters with teachers. The resulting material, aimed at teachers entering urban classrooms, will be published in spring 2003.[12]

What we hear from these students in the following excerpts necessarily reflects the language and issues of school—whether liking a teacher is important, who gets called on in class discussions, second chances, grades. And what they have to say, unvarnished and sometimes disturbing, is what makes teaching so difficult: students want to be known well but to maintain boundaries and privacy; they need an adult's help even when they cannot ask for it; they crave respect and success but acknowledge "we're still growing."

What students care about most, in other words, is their relationships with teachers. And the most successful of these, they tell us, sound very much like the youth-adult partnerships of youth development vernacular. Students yearn for teachers eager to engage them in a scrupulous give and take grounded in mutual respect and trust. In return, they offer what we most want from them: a determination to meet challenges, behave generously, and do their best work.

Here, in their own words, is some of what students have to say. With two million new teachers needed over the next decade and

60 percent of beginning teachers quitting the profession within their first five years, their advice could not be more important.

On respect and trust

In high school classrooms, respect and trust have everything to do with learning, and they must travel a two-way street between teacher and student:

There was this guy who coached track. If he told you to do twenty laps and the guys were complaining he would say: "Okay, do five." If you were tired, he would say, "Okay, you can stop." He would take you out for pizza after practice. He was a cool coach; they all loved him. But when the time for the meets came, they never won. So they got a new coach. The new coach, if he says, "Do fifty laps," and they say, "We don't wanna," he'll say, "Oh no? Then do fifty-two!" They hated him because he made them work so hard. But when the time for the meets came, they won every single time. They learned the difference between respecting and liking.

Being able to trust your teacher and be trusted is important. One student in my school was homeless. The principal wasn't like, "Let's go to your house and talk to your mom"; he was like, "If you need a safe place to stay, I know someone you can talk to." He doesn't want you to feel embarrassed. When they have teacher conferences, he does not tell other people private things you have told him. If you're gay, if you're getting beat up, if you're not eating, if you're dealing with identity problems, you can tell him because you know that it is affecting your work. You can talk about it with him, and he'll keep giving you chances even if you keep messing up.

What builds trust between teachers and students, and what breaks it down? Students know that by going to school, they are making a bargain, usually unspoken, with their teachers.[13] And the adults who win students' trust and respect are those perceived as painstakingly fair in carrying it out. Here is how students define it:

If you will . . .	*Then we will . . .*
Show you know and care about the material	Believe the material can be about important for us to learn
Treat us as smart and capable of challenging work	Feel respected and rise to the challenge of demanding work

Allow us increasing independence but agree with us on clear expectations

Model how to act when you or we make mistakes

Show respect for our differences of opinion and individual styles

Keep private anything personal we tell you

Learn to act responsibly on our own, though we will sometimes make mistakes in the process

Learn to take intellectual risks and learn to make amends when we behave badly

Let you limit some of our freedoms in the interest of the group

Trust you with information that could help you teach us better

From the very first day, students are alert to signals of whether the teacher will uphold it—and that will largely determine whether they will do their part:

He made us get involved. He won the respect of the class. He didn't give up on the students. We ended up learning.

On whether liking matters

Everyone likes some people better than others. But in general, students want teachers to put good teaching ahead of popularity. As long as teachers care about their material and students' learning, most will learn from teachers they may not like personally:

It's okay if kids hate you at first. If you care about your teaching, we'll get past that. We're not going to be receptive to someone so quickly; we're kind of young in our thinking.

To a certain extent, you have to have a personality that students respond to. But that doesn't mean you have to be our best friend, because that will cause our education to suffer. I hate to admit it, but respect and authority are part of the job. Kids expect adults to give us directions and boundaries, but it's a balance.

I don't like the way my math teacher teaches, but I know that the way he comes into a classroom, he wants the students to leave knowing math.

This makes me open my mind to what he has to say and how he's trying to say it.

I'm going to learn whether or not the teacher and I are friends. As long as a teacher is real and the student is real and they are acting in a respectful way, there can be a give-and-take relationship with information.

On whether teachers must like students

It's not as important for a teacher to like the students as it is for the students to think the teacher likes them. Students feel more comfortable and motivated in classes where they think the teacher likes them.

When teachers appear to like some students more than others, students feel uncomfortable, whether or not they count among the favored. Most would rather stay somewhere in the middle, not singled out for favor or disfavor:

My French teacher has a very disturbing habit of calling some of his students his "advanced" students. This gives those that are not "advanced" a feeling of lesser value, and feelings of anger come up. He creates a barrier between himself and students, and even between students in the class.

I would rather not know if I'm a teacher's favorite. It puts me in a weird position. When we're having a test or something, other students will come up to me and say, "Why don't you ask if we can not have it—she likes you."

Some students may not feel comfortable making a personal connection until after a course has ended:

When I'm their student, I go to them for help and nothing else—it's just something I have. After I'm not their student any more, I might go to them just to talk. I tell them how my new teacher is and how I like my new class.

On connections and boundaries

Students respect teachers who are comfortable with themselves. If teachers convey self-respect, students will respond, even when cultural differences seem immense:

Teachers have to not be afraid to show themselves and at the same time maintain a boundary. Don't try to look like me, talk like me, dress like me, put your hair in cornrows. The minute you try to broadcast about yourself in order to make a connection with the kid, that's the minute it fails, because we can sniff out that kind of thing. If you just keep teaching, you will eventually reach someone. We'll put in the effort to connect with you.

They want teachers to act like adults, confident and authoritative:

If you start as an authority figure, the relationships will come. You can get friendly later on. And you can be friendly and still be strict. You have to let them know that you're not one of their peers.

On taking risks

Taking a risk in class—by offering an opinion, venturing an answer without being sure, or showing how much they know—is especially hard for teenagers, who care so much about their peers' opinions:

Intimidation is invisible to a teacher in a classroom. They can't necessarily see that for whatever subject it is, every student often adds extra pressure to ourselves in our minds—not wanting to be picked on, people will make fun of you, you don't have the right answer. These are all the things that run through your mind, and your teacher doesn't know that that's the way you feel.

I'm working extra hard to know all the answers, and I'm then having to work extra hard so the other kids don't punish me for knowing all the answers. For the sake of the class running smoothly, you have to have someone to answer the question, but why every day! I think I've been a crutch for the teacher in at least 85 percent of my classes. I like knowing things, but whether or not I know it shouldn't make or break your class.

Whether they know the material, many students feel painfully reluctant to draw attention to themselves, but they want their teachers to look hard for possible openings:

Every student wants to feel special and smart and talented, but at the same time we want to blend in. So when we make that little effort to raise our hand—and it takes a lot of effort to like stand out—we need you to see it and, more than seeing it, to seek it. And if we stutter a little bit and have trouble getting it out, don't be quick with us, but support us.

Students with backgrounds and upbringings that are different from those of the teacher probably will not share the same reference points of history, literature, film, or other cultural narratives. A teacher should be alert for silence, distraction, or little signs of confusion that might indicate this unfamiliarity. Without drawing attention to any particular student, a teacher can provide a brief explanation to prevent a conversation from excluding anyone:

Teachers assume you know what they're talking about; they assume that you'll ask if you have a problem. I don't know what *Schindler's List* is.

Teachers can speak privately to students having trouble and, without humiliating them, explain their expectations and help find ways for students to meet them:

I don't like it when people stare in my grill [in my face]. That teacher came to me and said, "I understand your frustration, but I'm not going to leave you alone. You have to write down what you have to say, so that by the time we get to you, you have something to say and you won't have to make anyone wait and look at you." So now that's what I do, and it was one of the most important things I ever learned in my high school career.

On second chances

Adolescents do not always make school a top priority. They may be spending most of their time figuring out their own identities as young adults. They may be using their energy to cross daily barriers of language and culture. Negative experiences in the classroom may have convinced them that school offers nothing worthwhile or that they will never fit into the boxes it provides:

They shouldn't expect me always to do good. Sometimes you go through lots of stuff—if something happens in your family, you might not be going to school—and you don't know when that is going to be. It's important for a teacher to let you know that even if you don't do the very best this time, they still expect that you'll be able to in the future.

Especially at a time when students are becoming adults, they need some leeway to make mistakes:

Because of something that happened in ninth grade, one teacher won't sit down with me and talk to me about anything. So I do the same back to her: I don't smile at her or respect her. Teachers need to make allowance for the fact that we change from year to year and even from week to week. Sometimes I'm just acting hotheaded; I need to clear the air and then come back and apologize. I can acknowledge the things I do wrong.

But if a teacher believes in students' value and ability, students are willing to try, and try again:

My algebra teacher when I got a C in his class, he was upset. He just pushed me to keep my head out them boys and into the books. He made me go to tutoring after school to keep my grades up.

When teachers consistently give this message, a culture of success begins to develop in the class and the school:

In my school, there's no one that's better than anyone else—we're all trying to graduate. You can stop a teacher and ask a question any time.

On grading and praising

By high school, teenagers see grades as a powerful and personal judgment on who they are and what their future may hold. A bad grade can feel like a debilitating blow; a good grade can boost their energy and motivation:

I hurt when I get a bad grade! You feel like you're doing all that hard work for nothing. Then you don't want to work more if you're just going to get bad grades. Whenever my grades get low, I feel like dropping out of school.

The one time I loved school was in the fifth grade when I got straight As on my report card. That was the most wonderful day.

Direct and specific feedback from the teacher helps more than grades:

You don't need to have grades to want to work harder. If my teachers told me how I was doing without grades, I would pay attention to it. You want to know how you're doing, but you don't want to feel bad about yourself. Just say, "I want you to do this, this, this, and this." They would be treating us more with respect.

But that feedback, particularly criticism, should remain private. Making students' grades public creates especially bad feelings:

Trading tests to correct them is embarrassing sometimes. We have a lot of students who can barely speak English, and she would call out, "Who got them all right? Who got less than ten?" And everyone knew what you got.

When the teacher tells me what I did wrong in front of the class, I feel very bad and like I am not capable. But I don't mind being singled out for praise.

Some teenagers, though, are equally sensitive to public praise:

I know the other person's gonna hate me when I get praise and someone else doesn't.

Important as they may be, grades and praise are not the only incentives that matter. Students realize that learning has its own rewards—intellectual, pragmatic, and psychological:

You love school when it's interesting and when it makes you feel smart. Getting good grades can make you feel that way. But also when you know the teachers care about you and your future: "I'm going to see you in five years, and you'll be in college."

Marshaling student voices

As every educator knows, good teaching entails far more than basic intelligence and knowledge. It takes genuine curiosity about people and ideas. It requires courage to look honestly at what is and imagine what could be. It requires humility to admit one's mistakes and to keep trying. It requires empathy, to hear and feel what someone else is experiencing. And if these characteristics are true of good teaching, they also apply to genuine learning. For our forty student coauthors, these qualities emerged as cornerstones of what they valued in others and themselves.

Curiosity, humility, and mutuality were our guideposts too as we worked hard to draw out these students' experiences and together build a schema for teacher-student partnerships whose benefits might reach deep and touch all. Here is what we have learned about marshaling student voices:

* *Root the process in inquiry, asking questions both you and the students care about.* In our case, we needed to know what new teachers worried about most as they prepared to teach adolescents in diverse urban classrooms. We began by querying several groups of beginning teachers, "If you could ask your students any question about what or how you teach, what would you ask?"

From their replies, we shaped at least one hundred questions, sorting them into approximately thirty sets that seemed to go together. For example, new teachers expressed considerable anxiety about whether students would like them and whether a friendly relationship would challenge their authority. So we asked students to describe the teacher they liked the best and also the teacher from whom they learned the most. Were those two different, and if so, how and why?

We kept the questions concrete, basing them in students' experiences, not just their opinions. Not all our questions bore fruit. During uncomfortable pauses, we learned to ask, "Is this the right question? What do you think the real question is?" We asked students what questions we might be forgetting.

Steadily, students transformed our questions—that is, the questions of new teachers—into their own. For us, this was a crucial goal from the start: that the students be collaborators, not subjects, in the research.

* *Gather a group of students willing to express their thoughts.* Half of our students were recent immigrants, just learning English. The other half included students for whom school had been an off-and-on

affair (sometimes mostly off), along with a handful of students who worked hard to do well. A willingness to share their thoughts, wrestle with questions, and analyze the results united this otherwise diverse group.

• *Write everything down.* Our sessions combined talking and writing in proportion to students' capacities and rhythms. The facilitator recorded everything students said on a notebook computer, and we later transcribed students' handwritten responses to our question sets.

That visible commitment to take account of everything students said created a climate of purpose. The facilitator often read back what people had said for accuracy, asking follow-up questions and giving them the chance to critique, amend, or amplify their comments. A conversation that spiraled into personal chitchat returned more quickly to the subject as students saw their words written down.

• *Ask for evidence.* Because students are as ready as adults to engage in airy bull sessions, we continually sought supporting details in their responses. In a conversation about working in mixed groups, for instance, we pushed for specific situations in which students had struggled or succeeded. They grew used to our saying, "Can you tell me more about that?" or "What was that like for you?"

As students worked together, they also grew adept at supporting their own assertions and probing each other's experiences for nuance and contradictions. The fact that we had to write something from their responses sharpened the need to get it right. They began to acquire the habits of the journalist and the researcher, to look for pieces of the puzzle.

• *Analyze the material together.* Because our goal was to offer advice, our discussions always ended with, "So what would you suggest to a teacher?" Analyzing the suggestions together, we created lists of do's and don'ts, questionnaires, calendars, and exercises to help teachers and students better understand each other. We weighed whether spontaneous advice ("We shouldn't have homework!") was merely frivolous or contained kernels of wisdom.

Encouragingly, students' suggestions often derived from the example of a particularly effective teacher in their school. Again and again, students testified to the power of a teacher to change not just their minds but also their lives.

Nobody ever asked us that before

It is tempting to think that if you just pay attention to students' voices, you will hear what you already know. Secretly, adults—outside schools as well as in—generally believe that they know best. Just as tempting is to take at face value the quick responses students often give when asked for input. As we know but too often forget, some students feed back what they think adult listeners want to hear, some feel ill-qualified to render an opinion, and some fear reprisal for speaking what they believe is true. Hardest of all, some students, even when encouraged, keep their feelings under close wrap.

If we are to make student voices matter, to take seriously the notion of student-teacher partnerships, we must do several things. First, we must make time and room for them in our daily lessons, ceding the floor and agenda to matters of importance to them. Second, as we draw out student voices, we must listen respectfully and hard, including probing silences to uncover what goes unsaid. Finally, we must make the translations: turning students' ideas and experiences into new understandings that generate new practice. We must make the unspoken bargain struck by students and teachers an explicit partnership in which both parties acknowledge a common stake. We must accept as a given, not just pay lip service to, the idea of students as allies. Despite an adolescent culture that often suggests otherwise, students already recognize the symbiotic nature of education. If only from self-interest, they want their teachers to succeed. "We *want* to learn," one student reminded us. Such actions not only teach and mirror the processes of inquiry and reflection that animate the best classrooms, but also the notion of partnership itself.

At the end of one long day's work, we asked our student collaborators, "Has anyone ever asked you questions like these before?"

Their heads shook no. Both students and teachers will gain when we right this silence.

Notes

1. Dollar, B., with Kleinbard, P., & Randall, K. (1975). *Youth participation: A concept paper.* New York: National Commission on Resources for Youth.

2. Hoover, A. B., & Weisenbach, A. (1999). Youth leading now! Securing a place at the table. *New Designs for Youth Development, 15*(3), 30.

3. Princeton Survey Associates. (1998). *Young People's Community Involvement Survey: Report on the findings.* New York: Do Something.

4. Irby, M., Ferber, T., & Pittman, K., with Tolman, J., & Yohalem, N. (2001). *Youth action: Youth contributing to communities.* Takoma Park, MD: Forum for Youth Investment, International Youth Foundation.

5. Bernard, B. (1996). *Resilience research: A foundation for youth development.* Washington, DC: National Network for Youth.

6. Mohamed, I., & Wheeler, W. (2001). *Broadening the bounds of youth development: Youth as engaged citizens.* New York: Ford Foundation and Innovation Center for Community and Youth Development; Cahill, M. (1997). *Youth development and community development: Promises and challenges of convergence.* Takoma Park, MD: Forum for Youth Investment, International Youth Forum; Roth, J., & Brooks-Gunn, J. (2000). *What do adolescents need for healthy development?* New York: W. T. Grant Foundation.

7. Gardner, J. W. (1986). *Leadership development: Leadership papers.* Washington, DC: INDEPENDENT SECTOR.

8. Zeldin, S., McDaniel, A. K., Topitzes, D., & Calvert, M. (2000). *Youth decision-making: A study on the impacts of youth on adults and organizations.* Minneapolis: University of Wisconsin-Madison, with the Innovation Center for Community and Youth Development and the National 4-H Council.

9. Mohamed & Wheeler (2001).

10. *MetLife Survey of the American Teacher.* (2000, 2001). New York: MetLife.

11. What Kids Can Do worked with forty student collaborators, aged fifteen to eighteen, in New York City, San Francisco, Oakland, California, and Providence, Rhode Island. They attend (or have in the past) large, failing middle and high schools, progressive small schools, and a few private schools. Their classroom experiences and academic records vary just as widely. Several have been quite successful, seeking and winning full-time scholarships to well-regarded independent schools; others have moved in and out of school, dropping out of one and returning to another; some have worked hard but fall short of being classroom stars; many of the recent immigrants are still sorting out their paths as students. Colleagues in the four cities (where we also enlisted a higher education partner) helped recruit our student collaborators, those who would both contribute to and gain from the intensive three- to four-day writing workshops we conducted in each city.

12. Cushman, K., & the Students of What Kids Can Do. (forthcoming). *Fires in the bathroom: Advice for teachers from high school students.* New York: New Press.

13. We are grateful to Joseph McDonald for his framing of "the deal" between students and teachers (unpublished paper, 2001). It offered an invaluable lens through which these students explored and analyzed their experiences.

BARBARA CERVONE *and* KATHLEEN CUSHMAN *are cofounders of What Kids Can Do, a nonprofit organization that brings national attention to the voices, work, and community contributions of young people. Together, they combine forty years of experience in supporting adolescent learning in and outside school.*

Youth evaluators describe their findings from an extensive evaluation of forty youth programs in San Francisco. Interviews with current youth and the former program director provide insight into the promise and challenge of youth participation.

6

Youth evaluating programs for youth: Stories of Youth IMPACT

In 2000, the San Francisco Department of Children Youth and Their Families (DCYF) worked with local nonprofit organizations to involve youth in the evaluation of city-funded services for youth. The youth research team that took shape, Youth IMPACT, conducted an extensive evaluation of forty youth-serving programs in the city. In addition to analyzing and reporting their findings, Youth IMPACT developed a set of criteria that are now used to assess the quality of future grant applications. Youth IMPACT continues to work with the city to assess the quality of programs and resources for youth. This chapter presents excerpts from the report written by members of Youth IMPACT in 2001, an interview with four current members of Youth IMPACT, and an interview with Deborah Alvarez-Rodriguez, the former director of DCYF (now vice president for direct community experience with the Omidyar Foundation in California), who initiated the project.[1]

NEW DIRECTIONS FOR YOUTH DEVELOPMENT, NO. 96, WINTER 2002 © WILEY PERIODICALS, INC.

Youth evaluate: The Youth IMPACT report

Youth IMPACT's 2001 report, *Youth Voices Inspiring Creative Change*, was received with great excitement in the youth services community. Social service professionals and policymakers locally and nationally have been impressed not only by the deep concern for the community expressed by the youth authors but also by the careful research and useful findings that their evaluation produced. It began:

We are a group of San Francisco youth that represent the diversity of the city and were hired to do a city-wide evaluation of community based organizations (CBOs) funded by the Department of Children Youth and Their Families (DCYF). This publication was entirely written by us, with the help of adult staff in the final editing. Our goal was to help you get a better sense of what the youth need, so that you could improve the overall resources for youth in San Francisco. . . .

   Being youth ourselves, we found that in general, youth were more open to talking to us and being "real" with their feelings about their programs. Overall, we found that many of the CBOs are serving youth well and that youth are generally satisfied with their programs. However, there is always room for improvement. . . .

   Beginning in November 2000, we participated in trainings and activities that developed our skills in team building, personal development, public speaking, critical thinking and evaluation. During the Youth IMPACT process we went through four research phases in developing our Methodology. Our "methodology" describes the steps we took during each phase and how we did what we did. The first phase was the development of our research questions. The next was the development of our research instruments. Following this was the data collection phase. Then we did data analysis. Our last phase was coming up with recommendations and creating this publication.[2]

Youth IMPACT's guide to having the best CBOs

Youth IMPACT's research yielded positive findings about San Francisco's youth programs. The majority of the youth they interviewed reported having positive relationships with adult staff and felt that their lives had improved as a result of their involvement in the youth programs. However, the report also highlighted key areas for improvement:

There are still some things that can be improved in order for San Francisco to have the best CBOs. Here are our recommendations based on our research.

First of all, the biggest issue we saw while evaluating these programs was the lack of space. Many CBOs offered very good services to the youth and actually wanted to serve more youth, but there was no place to put them. In CBOs across the city it was the same thing; youth, staff, and supplies were often jammed into closet-like spaces. Also the programs sometimes had walls that looked very old and worn out. We believe that CBOs should add more space to their programs and if they already have sufficient space they should try to improve the condition of it. This may require extra funding from DCYF and other sources.

Pencils, paper, and pens . . . in this day and age a lot more supplies are required in order to have a GREAT CBO. We all know that computers are now a necessity in the 21st century. From the many CBOs that we visited we found that many of them had old computers (we are talking about the Apple Computers that they used in the Flintstones). Those CBOs that were lucky enough to have current computers were missing one major component: the internet. Many times we found that the internet was only available on one or two computers, and for programs with twenty or more participants this became a problem. So we suggest that the CBOs add more computers that are connected to the internet to their programs, and again this brings up money issues.

In addition to adding computers, we feel that the CBOs should try offering different classes at their sites. Even if youth come to your program for tutoring, it might be nice to have a conflict resolution class or even a cooking class so that the youth at your program have an opportunity to learn new things. Believe it or not, many of the people in the neighborhoods that we visited did not even know a CBO existed there. One way that CBOs can recruit more participants is by letting those in the community know where you are located and what type of services you offer. Try having an "Open House" where members of the community can come in and look at the facilities and meet your staff. Because what good is a GREAT CBO if no one knows it's there?

Unfortunately, while at the CBOs we sometimes noticed that staff were screaming or disrespecting the youth, and while doing our Focus Groups and looking at the questionnaires we found that a few youth had problems with the staff. One way to improve this is to offer more training to the staff. If staff are trained to avoid taking their anger out on youth even when they are having a bad day this will improve CBOs dramatically. Also staff should always take what a youth tells them seriously. It takes a lot of effort for a youth to approach an adult with their problems, and if they are laughed away they will not feel comfortable talking to the staff again. Always make sure that you let the youth at your program know that you are there if they ever need to talk. Even if they don't accept the offer to talk, it will make them feel good just knowing that you offered. Youth really want someone they can connect with so it helps to make sure that you have staff who share similar experiences with youth in the program or staff who come from the same community. Ageism is also a big problem. Even though staff are older than the youth they serve, they should not treat them as though they are inferior. We are youth and we have important things to say and we want to be treated with the same respect that we show you.

Snacks are the most important part of a program. After school we are starving and, believe it or not, we don't want chips all the time and we do get tired of drinking Kool-Aid. So please have snacks at your program and don't be afraid to try something different. Add some fruit or maybe even a pizza once in a while. Hey, you never know if we will like it if you don't try. If you try different snacks don't be surprised if more of the food ends up in the youth's mouths rather than the trash. Also, many kids might just start coming to your program because they hear from their friends that you have good snacks. Hey, free food works!

Lastly, the time your programs start. It is pretty hard to get to a program that starts at 3:20 when you get out of school at 3:15. Make your programs start later or at least let them run later so that all participants have enough time to fully enjoy the activities that are going on. Even try offering your program on weekends. You will be surprised how many youth will actually wander in.

Ah, the memories

As part of their report, Youth IMPACT members described the process of their getting involved and invested and what they learned along the way:

Many of us came into the program having no idea what we were actually going to do and then we sat through a long meeting in which it seemed as though they [the adults] were speaking a different language. What the heck was a CBO? Well eight months later we know that CBO stands for Community Based Organization and that we were hired to take part in one of the largest Youth Evaluations in the country. Youth IMPACT has become much more than a job. It changed many of our lives dramatically. The program has given us the opportunity to make new friends and enhance our writing and presentation skills. It has also taught us patience (sitting through long explanations about cross-tabulation). More importantly it has taught us not only how to work with people from different backgrounds, but how to get along with them. Those of us who came into the program shy and afraid of talking to people are now the main ones leading presentations to groups of over 100 people. We all feel that this job is an exceptional one. How many youth can tell their friends that they are working with the Department of Children, Youth and Their Families (DCYF) to improve the services of San Francisco? Well all of us at Youth IMPACT can.

During the year at this program we have had our eyes open to the issues that are prevalent throughout the city. We have found that although CBOs do have things that can be improved we believe that all of them have the interest of their youth in their hearts. We have all endured research questions, CBO meetings and staff changes, all the while adding the special Youth IMPACT "flava" to everything that we do. Thanks to the over 18 staff at Youth IMPACT for giving us total creative control of everything we produced and all of our presentations. Because of this we were able to have fun and handle our "biz" at the same time. We turned the usual uneventful evaluator and CBO meetings into a place where you can learn the information while having a good time, because who said that evaluating had to be boring or scary!

Beyond our personal benefits from the Youth IMPACT program we feel that it benefits the city of San Francisco; being youth ourselves we know what youth want and need. We also feel that the youth were more open talking to people who are their own age rather than adults. We hope that this final product and all of our findings and suggestions will be used to improve the youth programs of San Francisco.

We wish the Youth IMPACT team of 2001–2002 much luck and we want to tell them that even though at times you may feel like quitting because things are tiring or difficult, hang in there because in the end it is all worth it!

As this report excerpt shows, the young people of Youth IMPACT faced a number of challenges, but ultimately found that their efforts brought invaluable rewards.

Youth evaluators talk about Youth IMPACT

The best descriptions of the Youth IMPACT experience come from the youth evaluators themselves. In the following interview, current Youth IMPACT members discuss how youth participation can affect both their lives and the lives of their peers:[3]

INTERVIEWER: Tell me a little bit about what Youth IMPACT is.

MARVIN: Youth IMPACT started in 2000, basically to train youth in evaluating CBO programs for youth—because it makes sense that youth instead of adults evaluate their own programs. That way, they could find out more about what youth need because usually youth are kind of shy talking to adults. So that's why they thought it would be better to have youth evaluators.

INTERVIEWER: Have there been interviews that you've done where it seemed like youth have related to you differently because you were a young person?

MARVIN: Well, I don't know how they react to adults, but to us they really spoke their minds. They just told us everything that was going on—how they felt about their staff and everything. I don't think they would talk to an adult about their staff because they might think they would tell them or something.

INTERVIEWER: What are some techniques that you use to establish trust at the beginning of an interview?

ERIC: At the beginning, we talk to them and just get to know them and socialize with them a little bit to make them feel comfortable, so that it's not like a real serious thing—but in a way it is.

ELENA: Yeah, basically making it into a conversation form to let them know that you're not going to do anything wrong with the information they give you, and it's going to be important.

MARVIN: Well, you just let them know what's going on and what you're going to be doing. One big thing that helps is if you tell them that nobody else is going to get this information, just the group, so it's all confidential. That helps a lot.

INTERVIEWER: What about this project interested you or made you want to get involved?

ELENA: I wanted to work with youth. I wanted to experience that—helping them out, because I know there's a lot of programs that are not helpful. And I wanted to see why not and find a solution. Because there's a lot of youth that are hanging around in the city that . . . I don't like it. It's very dangerous. So I wanted to involve myself to help them out.

MARVIN: I didn't really know what Youth IMPACT was when I joined. I thought we were just going to be passing out papers and getting paid. But what made me keep going this year was that I thought it was better than working at McDonald's or something. I'd rather be with a group of people I liked instead of being somewhere cooking hamburgers.

INTERVIWER: How would you compare it to working at a fast food restaurant?

MARVIN: With this job, you actually have a future. And it helps you out applying to colleges and stuff. McDonald's is just like you learn how to cook burgers. That's it. That's not a career.

ERIC: So this basically helps you, *and* it also helps the youth around us in San Francisco to have better youth programs or after-school programs.

INTERVIEWER: What are some ways it helps you?

ERIC: The skills I've learned in Youth IMPACT carried indirectly to schoolwork and all sorts of stuff. At the beginning, before I joined Youth IMPACT, my public speaking skills weren't that good. I was a little shy at speaking in front of big groups. But since Youth IMPACT is about speaking all the time, that's made me feel more comfortable than before.

YULIMAR: The presentation skills have really helped me also.

ERIC: And some of the future things we might be doing is evaluation. I really don't think I can learn that from elsewhere.

INTERVIEWER: So can you tell me a little bit about the current project that you're working on this summer?

YULIMAR: We're working on an asset map to help youth in San Francisco find jobs. Basically, we're dividing the city into eleven districts and listing at least three jobs in each district that's a job with a future, a job with three or more skills that we have on our list—technical skills, interactive skills, and all that stuff.

INTERVIEWER: Can you give me an example of a job with a future?

YULIMAR: An internship at a nonprofit organization that would help you in the future.

ERIC: So basically what we're going to do is go out and research all the places that are hiring currently to see what type of jobs they have available. If they fit in our criteria, we'll put them on our list—and obviously we'll ask them for permission. Once we gather our list, we'll create a final product, which is the asset map.

INTERVIEWER: How did you guys decide that you wanted to do the asset map?

NISHI [STAFF MEMBER]: They were working on the community needs assessment before this, where they were just handing out surveys. And one of our youth, a senior named Audrey, was completely frustrated about the process. She said, "I don't understand how this is a community needs assessment. This is not how we should be doing it. What we *should* be doing is mapping the city and figuring out what resources are available for people. Because then you kind of can figure out what the needs are of that community." And so we thought, "Oh, there's an idea!" So it stemmed from her.

ERIC: Before, when I was looking for a job, it was really hard for me because I would go to one place and I would only see one or two jobs. And go to another and they might not even have any. So I'd go to ten different places before I could even find a couple jobs that were available. So, to me, it would be very helpful to have a list of jobs by district or by the area.

INTERVIEWER: What are some challenges involved with youth and adult partnerships?

YULIMAR: Sometimes it's hard to see the other person's point of view because of the age difference. There may be conflicts on how you're going to go about getting something done.

ERIC: That's really the case sometimes. I think if both sides—the youth and the adults—are open-minded, then things could be worked out. Sometimes the adult can give the youth a lot of their own past experience and advice that we wouldn't probably think of.

And we have our values—what youth are thinking about and what we need and stuff. The most successful programs have a good group of people that is dedicated to learn and to do things.

YULIMAR: And if the adults are really trying to put youth in leadership roles, there are times when they need to step back and let the youth take initiative and let them lead.

INTERVIEWER: Can you give me an example of a time when that would be appropriate?

YULIMAR: If there was a presentation or something and the youth was supposed to present, but then they weren't really sure about what to say, the adults could help them—not really tell them what to say, but just help them process what they're trying to say.

ELENA: Give them some examples.

YULIMAR: Yeah. Just give guidance. Give their experiences, but don't tell them exactly what to do.

ERIC: Instead of saying it for us, just give us guidance on how to say it. Give examples of what are some good ways to say it and what are some of the things that you should probably include. But the final product should come from the youth's point of view.

MARVIN: The adult and youth relationships should both be equal. Because let's say the adult helps you out and stuff, but he's mean, or she's mean. That's not going to work out because that's kind of like forcing them to do it. You have to find the right adults to work with youth.

INTERVIEWER: Have you been in a youth program where they said, "Oh, we want to empower young people," but then actually it didn't turn out that way in reality?

ELENA: We were supposed to come up with a survey and community needs assessment. But they just gave us the surveys to play around with and change the questions to youth-friendly questions.

MARVIN: And they called it "youth led."

ELENA: Yes. Youth led. They said, "Okay, just change the words." And we didn't get to put any of the questions that we wanted. So that was really bad.

MARVIN: And we actually didn't find out they called it "youth led" until after the whole thing. It was like they told us, "Oh, just make it youth friendly," so we thought, "Oh, it's their survey; we just have to make it youth friendly." And they said it was part of our work, but we didn't really accept that.

YULIMAR: They just gave it to us and said, "Okay, pass these out. And we need this many by this date in each district."

MARVIN: Yeah. That just felt to me like a waste of time.

INTERVIEWER: What's the difference, then, between "youth friendly" and "youth led"?

YULIMAR: They asked us to make the questions youth friendly so that youth could relate to them and could understand what we were trying to ask. And "youth led" is us leading the entire process. Us writing the actual survey, taking it out, processing the data. Because we don't really know what happened afterward with all the surveys we collected.

MARVIN: They just told us that it would happen. But they didn't tell us the results.

INTERVIEWER: Is that how you would describe the asset mapping now?

YULIMAR: No. This *is* actually youth led. We're in a partnership with the adults.

ERIC: We're actually taking initiative in doing things like the focus groups and research of who to contact and what are some of the criteria that we want to use to find jobs.

ELENA: We're saying who we want to call, when we want to call, and what we want for youth.

ERIC: With the help of adults.

MARVIN: We're basically doing the work that we want to do— with a little bit of help from the adults.

YULIMAR: And not what they're telling us to do.

MARVIN: They give us options to choose, or we make options and we choose.

INTERVIEWER: One way that a reader could interpret this conversation is that you are saying that youth should be put in places where they do everything on their own and adults should just get out of the way.

ERIC: Not really, no. That's not what we're saying.

MARVIN: There should be a partnership.

ERIC: There should be equal partnerships among adults and youth.

MARVIN: No ageism.

ERIC: Yeah. And be respectful on both ends.

INTERVIEWER: Are there any other things that are important in terms of engaging youth in this kind of work?

YULIMAR: If we're targeting youth that you want to be hard working and dedicated like that, you should offer the skills that you think will help them in the future. For example, when I was applying to Youth IMPACT, they listed skills you learn, like presentation skills, evaluation skills—stuff like that.

MARVIN: So that youth would benefit.

ERIC: And another important thing would be having the right times. Make sure you pick a time where youth are able to work. Don't pick it at noon where they're still at school, or obviously you're not going to get any youth at all. No matter how much they want to work, if they can't get there by that time, then they can't work.

The foundations of Youth IMPACT: An interview with the former director

The Youth IMPACT project involved not only working with youth as community leaders, but also teaching adults to cooperate in youth-led projects. In the following interview, Deborah Alvarez-Rodriguez, former director of the San Francisco DCYF, describes the creation and ongoing evolution of Youth IMPACT, how it affected DCYF and its thinking about youth involvement, and recommendations for other communities interested in nurturing effective youth participation.[4]

INTERVIEWER: How did the idea for Youth IMPACT get started?

ALVAREZ-RODRIGUEZ: Youth IMPACT was created as part of a larger strategy to develop a set of standards and outcomes around children and youth in San Francisco. We wanted to create a baseline of currently available services and develop a set of tools to measure their quality and impact. As part of this, we felt we needed to blend the best of academic research, current best practices, with community participatory research, which included youth because they were a major stakeholder.

INTERVIEWER: Were people generally supportive of including youth?

ALVAREZ-RODRIGUEZ: We had a lot of convincing to do. I worked with the mayor to assure him that money set aside for planning and evaluation was an important and valuable public policy position to take, that this was a critical part of making sure that our young people get the kind of quality programming that they deserve. Then my budget had to go before the Board of Supervisors, and some members were quite supportive and others felt it was wasteful. This project was pretty unprecedented, and they just didn't know. Was it going to be biased? But eventually we had almost unanimous support from the board.

Actually, a few folks in the research field—in the youth development research field no less—had this attitude that the youth should be trained in administering adult-designed instruments. I was very adamant that that was not going to happen here. The adults participating in the project were to be mentors and coaches, but it was the *youth* who were the researchers and architects. And that took a little back-and-forth, and periodically we would have to remind folks that that was the intent.

INTERVIEWER: Going into the project, what were your main hopes for including youth?

ALVAREZ-RODRIGUEZ: One was that youth, who are traditionally marginalized in this society, were going to be at the table defining the questions. We were going to open the door and invite young people in—not for representation or to be one voice in a sea of adults or to rubber-stamp anything we were doing. They were there to formulate core research questions and thinking. I had a belief that they may just come up with something really different. And even if they came up with exactly the same thing, that would have been fine.

The other was that I wanted to fundamentally change the dynamics of power in San Francisco. Good government is being in partnership with your community. Part of that is having young people themselves transforming data into knowledge, and by doing that they had an opportunity to be at the table helping to set public policy.

INTERVIEWER: Did you have any fears going into the project?

ALVAREZ-RODRIGUEZ: Oh yeah! Our office was committing a fairly substantial amount of money with not a lot of definition around the project because we wanted the young people themselves to start defining it. You don't put out $200,000 to $250,000 with very little definition and not have anxiety about it!

The other thing was just trying to figure out how we were really going to manage this because I didn't want it to be a "youth program." I had to remind my staff and the consulting team and the young people themselves that this was a consulting engagement, they were experts, and they were to treat it with the level of professionalism—and I'm not talking about just the youth, *everybody* involved in this—and the level of quality that I expect from *any* expert consultant I'm hiring to help me and my staff learn and make decisions. There were a lot of challenges around making that transition in thinking.

Finally, I had to think about who on my staff could work well with both the over-eighteen consultants on the project and the under-eighteen consultants. Honestly, I didn't have the skills or the time to do it, and the majority of my staff didn't either. We were very fortunate that I had brought in a young woman who had done some youth-led, youth empowerment programming, but who also understood how data can be used to affect public policy. And I had a full-time intern who was spending a year in my office, and Youth IMPACT became her full-time job.

INTERVIEWER: In what ways do you feel like the project actually had an impact?

ALVAREZ-RODRIGUEZ: On so many levels. First of all, it clearly had an impact on those young people themselves. How they look at themselves, how they experience themselves in the world and in the context of leadership, was totally changed through this experience. How they view government was totally changed. So that was one.

Second, it transformed the service provider community, the youth-serving agencies. They had been leery initially, but as the Youth IMPACTers were visiting the centers and the different programs, doing the surveys, observations, and focus groups, and then presenting back to two hundred providers at a time in these large-scale seminars, the youth service community got engaged and started seeing the power and the benefit of this to them and what they were trying to do. This opened up their eyes that there was a whole other talent pool out there that they really weren't tapping, that could improve their work and help them meet their mission.

At DCYF, some folks became totally convinced that this was the way to go. There are still some naysayers, but overall the department shifted its whole work orientation to have youth as partners. We always had a youth employment program in our office, and they'd do some filing or something, but the notion of young people changed. It shifted away from menial things. On any given day now in this governmental office, you would see anywhere from four to seven youth doing essential jobs in the department. We had youth interns in the Planning Department helping to design focus groups for our community planning workshops and actually facilitating those workshops.

It also transformed our grant making. For example, the Ten Commandments of a Good Youth Program [developed by Youth IMPACT] are now part of every Request for Proposal. And there are actually criteria and measurement against that. And the amount of dollars set aside for youth-led programming increased substantially, to the point where there is now a mandated set-aside in the children's fund that 3 percent of all dollars have to be committed to youth-led programming. The actual allocation is even higher than that.

And young people became an integral part of the allocation process. Every review panel that looks at proposals has two young people assigned to it, actively participating in making decisions about where our money goes. Youth are members of the community advisory panel that guides the department. By legislation, we only had to have two youth representatives; we had *five*. Thirteen representatives, and five or six are young people.

Then other city departments started saying, "Hey! How can I do something like that? Is it possible for Youth IMPACT to design an evaluation for my department?" I don't know where that's going, if that's happening or not, but that was very much on the agenda.

INTERVIEWER: It seems like a lot of youth participation efforts struggle to become more than something tokenistic or involving youth in, as you said, rubber-stamping. What do you think made it possible for Youth IMPACT to be different, to get beyond that challenge?

ALVAREZ-RODRIGUEZ: Initially, it was commitment from the management team of the department to say, "You know, we will be changed. We will be forced into behaving and working differently. We don't know what that's going to look like and what it's going to mean, but we cannot go through this process and not expect to be affected." We had a great management team that really believed that this was the right thing to do and this would make their jobs better at the end of the day. And this is where, honestly, leadership at the top really did make a difference because when the going got tough—and let me tell you, the going has gotten tough on several occasions with Youth IMPACT—nobody said, "Let's throw it away." We were like, "No, let's sit down. Let's understand what is going on."

INTERVIEWER: If you were to take a step back and speak from your experience, what would you say to people in other cities who are interested in including youth in this kind of way?

ALVAREZ-RODRIGUEZ: The strongest reason for doing this is that you'll be able to develop better programs, better quality service, better public policy, better delivery systems for young people. That's just the bottom line: you will do a better job. Period. There's not any hesitation in my mind about that.

But it takes time and needs to be well resourced. Part of the challenge with Youth IMPACT in year one was that the time frame was too short, and we needed to extend it, and we're still trying to find out what's the right time frame to do this work. And it costs money. You've got to pay the young people well, the way you would pay someone else doing this!

You've got to make sure you have the right people managing it from inside your department and inside your organization because it takes particular kinds of skills and talents to manage this well. And most folks don't have that combination.

Be ready to be changed! You cannot do this work and think that you and your department and your service providers will be able to do business as usual. You have got to be willing to be changed. And if you're not, then don't do this.

And you need to respect the process of the young people as they go through this. Sometimes I saw people saying, "Oh, but they're young, and we shouldn't push them so hard. And, well, they've got a whole different fashion sense." Well, when they were presenting to me, I was the client. You don't come in clicking your gum or using profanity. There are standards of professional conduct and quality research. At the end of the day, I think the youth really appreciated it. I had a very good rapport with the majority of the young people, and I was frank. They'd do a presentation, and we'd go over the content of the presentation, but then I'd also give them feedback on style too. You have to understand that they're young and they don't have the life experience that other people do, but also don't use that as an excuse for poor quality or low expectations.

I think every community in America should have a participatory youth-led model, and not just with evaluation, but with their strategic planning—everything. When adults stop and listen—really listen—to what young people have to say and contribute, it is absolutely extraordinary what young people add to society, to their peers, to their adult counterparts. We have got to create thousands of mechanisms to engage young people in a real partnership. And

I say that not just because of *their* future, but I feel like *my* future is in jeopardy if we don't do that.

Notes

1. During its first year, which the report is based on, Youth IMPACT was a collaboration between the Department of Children, Youth and Their Families (DCYF), JMPT Consulting, and Youth in Focus. JMPT Consulting specializes in technology and policy. Youth in Focus is a nonprofit training and consulting organization dedicated to youth empowerment, organizational improvement, and community development through supporting youth-led research, evaluation, and planning. Currently, Youth IMPACT is a collaboration between DCYF and Literacy for Environmental Justice (LEJ), a nonprofit youth development organization aiming to foster an understanding of environmental justice and urban sustainability.

2. A more detailed discussion of Youth IMPACT's methods and results is available at http://www.dcyf.org/307_publications.htm.

3. The interview was conducted by Benjamin Kirshner on July 17, 2002. Three of the youth speakers, Yulimar, Eric, and Elena, are in their first year with Youth IMPACT and are starting their senior year in high school. The fourth youth, Marvin, joined Youth IMPACT in 2000 as a high school senior and is now in his second year at City College of San Francisco. The adult staff person, Nishi Moonka, started at LEJ in the winter of 2002.

4. The interview was conducted by Jennifer O'Donoghue on June 27, 2002.

Index

Adults: HOME Project program for staff development of, 25n.27; youth stakeholders in partnership with, 85–86. *See also* Teachers
Alvarez-Rodriguez, D., 18, 21, 101, 111–117
Awareness raising letter-writing theme, 58–59

Bagby, M., 67
Bantu education system protests (South Africa), 31
Blood Reserve (Alberta), 52
Brazilian street children's movement, 42
Brooks-Gunn, J., 29

California Fund for Youth Organizing, 43
California youth political protests, 32
Cammarota, J., 34
Centre of Excellence for Youth Engagement, 47, 61
Cervone, B., 6, 11, 83, 99
Chevron Corporation, 39
Class participation: marshaling student voices in, 94–97; role of respect and trust in, 88–89; role of teacher popularity in, 89–90; student grading and praising and, 93–94; student risk taking and, 91–92; student second chances and, 92–93; student voice in, 87; student-teacher connections and boundaries and, 90–91; teacher liking for students and, 90. *See also* Student participation
Collective action: creating system change through, 38–39; encouraging, 36–37
Community: benefits of youth participation for, 84–86; conceptual

framework for youth engagement in, 48–50; decision making for engaging in life of, 47–48; Effective Citizenry's community problem solving, 69–71; impact of youth participation on, 18–19; SJYD outcome focus on well-being of, 41–42; SJYD support of problem solving for, 41; youth civic activism changing the, 74
CRC (United Nations Convention on the Rights of the Child), 15–16, 32
Creating Change 2001, 52–53
Cushman, K., 6, 11, 12, 83, 87, 99

Data Center (California), 78–79
DCYF (San Francisco Department of Children Youth and Their Families), 12, 101, 105, 114
Decision making: development of, 41; engaging in life of community through, 47–48
Diallo, A., 32–33
duBois, P., 71

Effective Citizenry (Surdna Foundation): deeper levels of youth participation adopted by, 80; description of, 66–67; direct problem solving action by, 69–71; moral exploration by youth encouraged by, 74–75; promotion of youth public life by, 66–71; two-pronged funding approach by, 11, 67–69
Empowerment letter-writing theme, 58

Funders Collaborative on Youth Organizing, 79

119

Garbarino, J., 28
George Peabody Award for Excellence
    in Journalism, 77
Ginwright, S., 5, 9, 27, 34, 46

Hazen, E. W., 43
Hazen Foundation, 40
Healing development, 41
Health Canada, 47
Hilton Hotel, 39
HOME Project: adult staff develop-
    ment by, 25n.27; public life
    engagement through, 72–73
Hope for the future letter-writing
    theme, 59

Identity. See Youth identity
Institutional practices: creating systemic
    change through collective action,
    38–39; embedding youth participa-
    tion into, 18; encouraging youth
    civic activism, 74; promoting sys-
    temic change in, 36
INTERRUPT's Youth Media Council,
    77

Jagers, R. J., 34
James, T., 5, 9, 27, 46
John W. Gardner Center for Youth and
    Their Communities, 79
Juvenile offenses penalties (California),
    19, 29, 32, 39, 45n.12

Kids Can Do, 12
Kirshner, B., 2, 7, 9, 15, 26
KTUV (San Francisco), 77

LA Youth, 77
Lappe, F., 71
LISTEN (Local Initiative Support,
    Training, and Education Network)
    Inc., 37, 45n.16, 78
Loiselle, L., 6, 10, 47, 64
Los Angeles Times, 77

McLaughlin, M., 2, 7, 9, 15, 26
Males, M., 30
Media coverage, 76–78

MetLife Foundation, 87
Minority youth. See Urban youth of
    color

Nakamura, J., 48, 49
National Commission on Resources for
    Youth, 83
National Funder Collaborative on
    Youth Organizing, 43
New York City youth political protests,
    32–33
New York Times, 77
Noam, G. G., 3

O'Donoghue, J. L., 2, 7, 9, 15
Omidyar Foundation (California), 101
Optimist Clubs, 52

Pancer, S. M., 6, 10, 47, 49, 64
Peer Resources (San Francisco Educa-
    tion Fund), 67–69
Personal growth letter-writing theme,
    58
Philadelphia Student Union, 76
Philadelphia youth organizing groups,
    32
Pittman, K., 84
Power: developing tools to analyze, 37;
    social relationships and, 36; as
    youth participation component,
    2–3
Pratt, M. W., 49
Problem solving: Effective Citizenry's
    action for community, 69–71;
    SJYD support of social and com-
    munity, 41; youth political partici-
    pation and, 37–38
Proposition 21 (California), 19, 29, 32,
    39, 45n.12
Proposition 187 (California), 29
Proposition 209 (California), 29
Proposition 227 (California), 29

The Quickening of America (Lappe and
    duBois), 71

Rights of the Child (UN Convention),
    15

Romix Corporation, 75
Rose-Krasnor, L., 6, 10, 47, 64

San Francisco Board of Education, 69
San Francisco Examiner, 77
Self-awareness letter-writing theme,
    58
Sherman, R. F., 6, 11, 65, 82
SJYD outcomes: sociopolitical compe-
    tencies supported by, 41–42;
    unique nature of, 40–51
SJYD practices: building youth identity,
    38; creating systemic change
    through collective action, 38–39;
    developing tools to analyze power
    and problem-solving, 37–38; using
    youth culture to involve youth
    politically, 39–40
SJYD principles: analyzing power
    within social relationships, 36;
    embracing youth culture, 37;
    encouraging collective action,
    36–37; making identity central,
    36; promoting systemic change,
    36
SJYD (social justice youth develop-
    ment): examining, 5–6; increasing
    investment in, 42–44; joining exist-
    ing collaboration using, 43; princi-
    ples of, 35–40; principles, practices,
    outcomes of, 34*t*–35*t*, 36–42; sup-
    porting initiatives of, 43; value of
    examining, 33–34. *See also* Youth
    political participation
Social relations (fun and friendship) let-
    ter-writing theme, 59
Social relations (values and beliefs) let-
    ter-writing theme, 59–60
Social relationships, analyzing power
    within, 36
"Social toxins," 28–29
Sociopolitical development and analysis,
    41
South African Bantu education system
    protests, 31
Spiritual development, 41
Student participation: commitment to,
    1–2; disillusionment with, 1–2, 3;
    examples of existing, 86–88. *See also*
    Class participation

Student voices: class participation and,
    87; marshaling, 94–97; taken seri-
    ously by teachers, 97–98
Students: building trust between teach-
    ers and, 88–89; class participation
    and risk taking by, 91–92; connec-
    tions and boundaries between
    teachers and, 90–91; decision mak-
    ing disillusionment by, 1–2, 3;
    grading and praising of, 93–94; sec-
    ond chances for, 92–93; survey
    (2001) on trust by, 86; teacher lik-
    ing for, 90; teacher popularity and,
    89–90. *See also* Teachers
Students Commission (Canada): core
    values of, 53–54; feedback collec-
    tion by, 54; objectives, purposes,
    outcomes of, 61; youth conferences
    conducted by, 51–52, 53
Sullivan, L., 37
Surdna Foundation: collaboration with
    Peer Resources, 67–69; Effective
    Citizenry of, 11, 66–71, 74–75, 80
Systematic change: collective action to
    create, 38–39; promotion of, 36;
    through youth civic activism, 74

Teachers: building trust between stu-
    dents and, 88–89; connections and
    boundaries between students and,
    90–91; marshaling student voices,
    94–97; popularity and teaching of,
    89–90; student grading and prais-
    ing by, 93–94; student risk taking
    and role of, 91–92; student second
    chances and role of, 92–93; taking
    student voices seriously, 97–98. *See
    also* Adults; Students
Ten Commandments of a Good Youth
    Program (Youth IMPACT), 114
Tiny Giant Magazine, 52
Tokenism youth participation, 20–21
Trust: classroom role of respect and,
    88–89; student survey (2001) on,
    86

United Nations Convention on the
    Rights of the Child (CRC), 15–16,
    32
University of Wisconsin, 85

Urban youth of color: economic context of, 30; examples of political actions by, 31–33; political context of, 29–30; referred to as "social toxins," 28–29; social context of, 30–31; social-ecological approach to, 29; uncovering the assault on, 28–29

Vital engagement, 48–49

Watts, R. J., 34
We INTERRUPT This Message (San Francisco Bay Area), 77
We've Got Issues (Bagby), 67
What Kids Can Do, 87, 98n.11
Williams, N. C., 34, 40

Youth: media coverage and, 76–78; moral exploration by, 74–75; Proposition 21 increasing criminalization for, 19, 29, 32, 39, 45n.12; public lives of, 65–80; urban youth of color, 28–33
Youth conference letter-writing themes: awareness raising, 58–59; empowerment, 58; hope for the future, 59; self-awareness and personal growth, 58; social relations (fun and friendship), 59; social relations (values and beliefs), 59–60
Youth conferences: analysis and discussion of, 60–62; letter-writing themes of, 58–60; narrative description of, 54–57; research and evaluation of, 53–54; value of conducting, 51–53
Youth culture: used to involve youth politically, 39–40; value of embracing, 37
Youth development: civic activism as effective, 73–74; decision making, 41; using developmental framework for, 44; healing and spiritual, 41
Youth engagement: decision making for, 47–48; definition of and conceptual framework for, 48–50; outcomes of, 50–51; political development and, 27–28, 31–42,

34*t*–35*t*; vital engagement and, 48–49; youth conferences and, 51–62
Youth engagement framework, 49*fig*
Youth identity: building, 38; as starting point for participation, 36
Youth IMPACT: adult role in, 21–22; collaboration with other organizations by, 117n.1; evaluation of youth services by, 12; examining, 6–7; grant application criteria developed by, 101; interview with former director of, 111–117; Ten Commandments of a Good Youth Program developed by, 114; *Youth Voices Inspiring Creative Change* report (2001) by, 13, 102–111
Youth participation: benefits of, 84–86; definition of, 5; future of, 23–24; impact on organizations and community by, 18–19; institutionalization of effective, 18; myths of, 19–23; power component of, 2–3; in research and practice, 16–19; student, 1–2, 88–98; UN CRC on fundamental right of, 15–16; youth stakeholders created from, 85–86
Youth participation myths: on adults being ready for youth participation, 22–23; impact on public policy decisions by, 19–20; as meaning adult surrender of guide and education roles, 21–22; on readiness of youth for participation, 23; on youth placement on board and committee, 20–21
Youth political participation: examples of, 31–33; social justice development principles and practices and, 33–42, 34*t*–35*t*; three fundamental questions on, 27–28. *See also* SJYD (social justice youth development)
Youth public lives: asking the right questions to encourage, 80; civic activism of, 73–74; Effective Citizenry's promotion of, 66–71; encouraging deeper levels of participation in, 79–80; examples of, 71–73; identity development through active, 74–75; media cov-

erage of, 76–78; promoting timely involvement in, 75–76; questions on how to promote, 65–66; strong youth-led organization and, 78–79
Youth Radio (California), 77
Youth Voices Inspiring Creative Change (Youth IMPACT): evaluation findings of, 13, 102; on guide to having best CBOs, 102–104; on process of involvement and investment by

participants, 104–105; youth evaluators on their experience with, 106–111, 117n.3
Youth-led organizations, 78–79
YouthNoise.com, 78
YUCA (Youth United for Community Action), 75, 76

Zeldin, S., 51

Back Issue/Subscription Order Form

Copy or detach and send to:
Jossey-Bass, A Wiley Company, 989 Market Street, San Francisco CA 94103-1741

Call or fax toll-free: Phone 888-378-2537; Fax 888-481-2665

Back Issues: Please send me the following issues at $28 each
(Important: please include issue ISBN)

_____

_____

$ _____   Total for single issues

$ _____   SHIPPING CHARGES: SURFACE   Domestic   Canadian
First Item $5.00 $6.00
Each Add'l Item $3.00 $1.50
Please call for next day, second day, or international shipping rates.

Subscriptions   Please ❑ start ❑ renew my subscription to _New Directions for Youth Development_ at the following rate:

U.S.	❑ Individual $75	❑ Institutional $149
Canada	❑ Individual $75	❑ Institutional $189
All Others	❑ Individual $99	❑ Institutional $223
Online Subscription		❑ Institutional $149

**For more information about online subscriptions visit
www.interscience.wiley.com**

-- _____   Are you eligible for our **Student Subscription Rate**? Attach a copy of your current Student Identification Card and deduct 20% from the regular subscription rate.

$ _____   Total single issues and subscriptions (Add appropriate sales tax for your state for single issue orders. No sales tax for U.S. subscriptions. Canadian residents, add GST for subscriptions and single issues.)

❑Payment enclosed (U.S. check or money order only)
❑VISA ❑ MC ❑ AmEx ❑ Discover Card #_____ Exp. Date _____
Your credit card payment will be charged to John Wiley & Sons.

Signature _____ · Day Phone _____
❑ Bill Me (U.S. institutional orders only. Purchase order required.)

Purchase order # _____
Federal Tax ID13559302   **GST 89102 8052**

Name _____

Address _____

_____

Phone _____ E-mail _____

PROMOTION CODE ND3

Other Titles Available

NEW DIRECTIONS FOR YOUTH DEVELOPMENT: THEORY, PRACTICE, AND RESEARCH
Gil G. Noam, Editor-in-Chief

YD95   **Pathways to Positive Development Among Diverse Youth**
Richard M. Lerner, Carl S. Taylor, Alexander von Eye
Positive youth development represents an emerging emphasis in
developmental thinking that is focused on the incredible potential
of adolescents to maintain healthy trajectories and develop resilience,
even in the face of myriad negative influences. This volume discusses
the theory, research, policy, and programs that take this strength-
based, positive development approach to diverse youth. Examines
theoretical ideas about the nature of positive youth development,
and about the related concepts of thriving and well-being, as well
as current and needed policy strategies, "best practice" in youth-
serving programs, and promising community-based efforts to mar-
shal the developmental assets of individuals and communities to
enhance thriving among youth.
ISBN 0-7879-6338-0

YD94   **Youth Development and After-School Time: A Tale of
Many Cities**
Gil G. Noam, Beth Miller
This issue looks at exciting citywide and cross-city initiatives in after-
school time. It presents case studies of youth-related work that
combines large-scale policy, developmental thinking, innovative
programming, as well as research and evaluation. Chapters discuss
efforts of community-based organizations, museums, universities,
schools, and clinics who are joining forces, sharing funding and other
resources and jointly creating a system of after-school care and
education.
ISBN 0-7879-6337-2

YD93   **A Critical View of Youth Mentoring**
Jean E. Rhodes
Mentoring has become an almost essential aspect of youth development and is expanding beyond the traditional one-to-one, volunteer,
community-based mentoring. This volume provides evidence of the
benefits of enduring high-quality mentoring programs, as well as
apprenticeships, advisories, and other relationship-based programs
that show considerable promise. Authors examine mentoring in the
workplace, teacher-student interaction, and the mentoring potential
of student advising programs. They also take a critical look at the
importance of youth-adult relationships and how a deeper under-

standing of these relationships can benefit youth mentoring. This issue raises important questions about relationship-based interventions and generates new perspectives on the role of adults in the lives of youth.

ISBN 0-7879-6294-5

YD92   **Zero Tolerance: Can Suspension and Expulsion Keep Schools Safe?**
Russell J. Skiba, Gil G. Noam
Addressing the problem of school violence and disruption requires thoughtful understanding of the complexity of the personal and systemic factors that increase the probability of violence, and designing interventions based on that understanding. This inaugural issue explores the effectiveness of zero tolerance as a tool for promoting school safety and improving student behavior and offer alternative strategies that work.

ISBN 0-7879-1441-X

NEW DIRECTIONS FOR YOUTH DEVELOPMENT
IS NOW AVAILABLE ONLINE AT WILEY INTERSCIENCE

What is Wiley InterScience?

Wiley InterScience is the dynamic online content service from John Wiley & Sons delivering the full text of over 300 leading scientific, technical, medical, and professional journals, plus major reference works, the acclaimed *Current Protocols* laboratory manuals, and even the full text of select Wiley print books online.

What are some special features of Wiley InterScience?

Wiley InterScience Alerts is a service that delivers table of contents via e-mail for any journal available on Wiley InterScience as soon as a new issue is published online.
Early View is Wiley's exclusive service presenting individual articles online as soon as they are ready, even before the release of the compiled print issue. These articles are complete, peer-reviewed, and citable.
CrossRef is the innovative multi-publisher reference linking system enabling readers to move seamlessly from a reference in a journal article to the cited publication, typically located on a different server and published by a different publisher.

How can I access Wiley InterScience?

Visit http://www.interscience.wiley.com

Guest Users can browse Wiley InterScience for unrestricted access to journal Tables of Contents and Article Abstracts, or use the powerful search engine.
Registered Users are provided with a *Personal Home Page* to store and manage customized alerts, searches, and links to favorite journals and articles. Additionally, Registered Users can view free Online Sample Issues and preview selected material from major reference works.
Licensed Customers are entitled to access full-text journal articles in PDF, with select journals also offering full-text HTML.

How do I become an Authorized User?

Authorized Users are individuals authorized by a paying Customer to have access to the journals in Wiley InterScience. For example, a university that subscribes to Wiley journals is considered to be the Customer. Faculty, staff and students authorized by the university to have access to those journals in Wiley InterScience are Authorized Users. Users should contact their Library for information on which Wiley journals they have access to in Wiley InterScience.